Justin Wilson's Easy Cookin'

Also by Justin Wilson

The Justin Wilson Cookbook

Justin Wilson #2 Cookbook: Cookin' Cajun

The Justin Wilson Gourmet and Gourmand Cookbook

Justin Wilson's Outdoor Cookin' with Inside Help

Justin Wilson's Homegrown Louisiana Cookin'

Justin Wilson Lookin' Back: A Cajun Cookbook

Justin Wilson's Easy Cookin'

150 Rib-Tickling Recipes for Good Eating

Justin Wilson

William Morrow and Company, Inc. / New York

It is the policy of William Morrow and Company, Inc., and its imprints and affiliates, recognizing the importance of preserving what has been written, to print the books we publish on acid-free paper, and we exert our best efforts to that end.

Library of Congress Cataloging-in-Publication Data

Wilson, Justin.
    [Easy cookin']
    Justin Wilson's easy cookin' : 150 rib-tickling recipes for good
eating / Justin Wilson. — 1st ed.
        p.   cm.
    Includes index.
    ISBN 0-688-15264-3
    1. Cookery, American—Louisiana style.   2. Cookery, Cajun.
3. Quick and easy cookery.   I. Title.
TX715.2.L68W549   1998
641.59763—dc21   97-36134
                                                                CIP

Printed in the United States of America

First Edition

2   3   4   5   6   7   8   9   10

ASSOCIATE EDITOR: SARAH SUE GOLDSMITH

BOOK DESIGN BY LAURA HOUGH

www.williammorrow.com

Contents

Introduction

Cooking is really easy when you love to cook. I just cook without plan and throw things together in such amounts as I think to be about right. The most difficult part of putting together this cookbook was actually writing it —pulling my recipes out of my head and putting them on paper with measured amounts.

I call this book *Easy Cookin'* because I've looked for ways to make my cooking even easier than it is. For example, I use a lot of herb salts and powders, such as onion, garlic, and celery, which eliminates a lot of peeling and choping. Some of the older Cajuns who've never heard of such stuff may frown on this newfangled cooking, maybe even my Momma, if she were still with us. Yet I never met a Cajun, young, old, or in-between, who didn't like the easy way of doing things. It's a way of life, taking it easy. That's how New Orleans, the Crescent City, got its present name—The Big Easy!

Justin Wilson's Easy Cookin'

Breakfast Foods

Breakfast to me is de mos' important meal of de day. Eat a

breakfast dat you will have your enjoys eatin'.

Corn Flour Pancakes

2 cups corn flour

½ teaspoon ground cinnamon

½ teaspoon salt

2 teaspoons baking soda

2 large eggs, well beaten

2 cups buttermilk

Olive oil

Mix the dry ingredients together real well in a large mixing bowl. Beat the eggs, then add the buttermilk to them. Mix well and add to the dry mixture.

Coat the bottom of a large frying pan with olive oil and heat up over a medium fire. Add the batter by the spoonful to the skillet and cook on both sides until golden brown. Serve with cane syrup or maple syrup.

Lost Bread

This is called lost bread because it's made with stale bread, which you might usually throw out. This lost bread can be eaten with honey, syrup, molasses, or jelly. It can also be eaten as a sandwich with whatever you like.

MAKES 3 SERVINGS

4 large eggs

½ cup dry white wine

A little salt

6 slices stale bread

½ cup (1 stick) margarine or butter

Beat the eggs together well and add the wine and salt, beating some more. Dip each slice of bread into the liquid, gently squeezing out the excess.

Melt the margarine in a large frying pan over a medium fire and fry each side of each soaked bread slice until golden brown. Add more margarine as needed to fry the bread.

Pecan Cornbread

Even people who don't like cornbread like this kind of cornbread. Easy to cook, easy to eat.

MAKES 8 TO 10 SERVINGS

3 tablespoons vegetable shortening or bacon
   drippings

2 cups cornmeal

1 cup all-purpose flour

1 cup pecan meal (you can find this in any
   good supermarket)

1 tablespoon salt

1 heaping teaspoon baking powder

1 heaping tablespoon baking soda

3 large eggs

2 cups buttermilk

Preheat the oven to 400 degrees. I cook this in two cast-iron frying pans, one large and one small. I put the shortening in the pans and put them in the oven while it is heating so the oil will be hot and ready to add to the cornmeal.

In a large mixing bowl, sift together the dry ingredients. In a small mixing bowl, beat the eggs and buttermilk together, then mix this with the dry ingredients, stirring well. Take the pans with the oil that has been heating in the oven, pour the oil into the batter, and stir immediately. Pour the batter back into the greased frying pans and bake until golden brown, about 50 minutes.

Turn the cornbread over and put it back in the oven for another 5 minutes. This is called "sweating" the cornbread.

Pecan Grits

MAKES 6 TO 8 SERVINGS

5½ cups water

1 cup regular grits

1 cup pecan meal

3 tablespoons margarine or butter

2 teaspoons salt

½ teaspoon cayenne pepper

Place 2 cups of the water in the bottom of a double boiler, turn the heat to medium-high, and let it come to a boil. Meanwhile, in the top of the double boiler, combine the remaining 3½ cups water, the grits, pecan meal, margarine, salt, and cayenne. Bring to a boil directly over a medium-high fire, stirring constantly. Turn the heat to low and continue cooking until the grits begin to thicken, about 20 minutes, stirring occasionally. Put the pot of grits on top of the boiling water, reduce the heat to low, and simmer for 30 minutes. Serve hot.

Scrambled Eggs with Cooked Rice

Actually, this is an egg jambalaya—and it's good.

MAKES 2 SERVINGS

2 extra-large eggs

2 tablespoons cooked long-grain rice

Salt and cayenne pepper to taste

A little onion powder

Olive oil

With a whisk, beat all the ingredients together real well. Cook, stirring, in an oiled frying pan over a medium fire until done the way you like and serve over toast.

Walnut Scrambled Eggs

MAKES 3 TO 4 SERVINGS

6 extra-large eggs

3 tablespoons ground walnuts

Salt and cayenne pepper to taste

Olive oil

Beat the eggs real well. Add the walnuts, salt, and cayenne and beat to combine. Heat a little olive oil in a large frying pan over a medium fire and cook the eggs, stirring, until done the way you like.

Appetizers

A lot of people like appetizers. Some even call dem nibbling foods or hors d'oeuvres. In fact, some people eat so many appetizers, dey don' need an entrée.

Pickled Eggs

I like to take a plain hard-boiled egg and a pickled egg and mash them up together to make an egg salad. Easy cookin'! The yield depends on who's hungry for pickled eggs.

24 large hard-boiled eggs, peeled

Vinegar, heated just below boiling

1 cup pimiento-stuffed olives, drained

½ cup jalapeño peppers, chopped

1 teaspoon dried mint

2 tablespoons onion powder

2 teaspoons garlic powder

Salt to taste

Place the eggs in a large jar with a tight-fitting lid. Add enough of the hot vinegar to cover the eggs. Place the rest of the ingredients in the jar, and cover tightly with the lid. Let them sit at room temperature at least 2 weeks; then someone can start eating them.

Crawfish or Shrimp Cocktail

MAKES 8 TO 10 SERVINGS, NO P-I-G HOGS

For the sauce:

½ **cup picante sauce**

1 **cup catsup**

½ **cup horseradish sauce**

1 **tablespoon Worcestershire sauce**

½ **teaspoon salt**

1 **tablespoon fresh lemon or lime juice**

½ **cup finely chopped fresh parsley**

Cayenne pepper to taste

8 **to** 10 **pounds peeled boiled crawfish or**

    shrimp (see page 75)

Combine all the sauce ingredients. Pour over the crawfish or shrimp or dip them in it.

Shrimp Pâté

Dis is better than you believe, that's how good it is.

MAKES 4 TO 6 SERVINGS

4 cups peeled boiled shrimp (see page 75)

1 cup pimiento-stuffed olives, drained

½ cup mild picante sauce

1 tablespoon horseradish sauce

Salt to taste

Put all the ingredients in a food processor and process until smooth. Chill and serve on crackers.

Oyster Pâté

MAKES 6 TO 8 SERVINGS

1 quart shucked oysters, with their juices

½ cup pimiento-stuffed olives, drained

Bacon drippings to taste

¼ teaspoon garlic powder

½ teaspoon onion powder

1 teaspoon chili powder

1 tablespoon dill relish, drained

¼ teaspoon cayenne pepper

1 tablespoon olive oil

1 tablespoon soy sauce

Salt to taste

Place the oysters and their juices in a medium-size pot and just cover with water. Bring to a boil.

Immediately drain the oysters and place in a food processor along with the remaining ingredients. Process until smooth, then chill and serve on crackers.

Alligator Pâté

Dis is very good pâté. Try it, you'll like it jus' as much as I do. Maybe you want to call it crocodile because you don' like alligator.

MAKES 6 TO 8 SERVINGS

For the alligator:

2 pounds cleaned (all the fat removed)
   alligator meat, cut up

To season the water:

1 tablespoon garlic powder

2 tablespoons onion powder

1 teaspoon dried mint

½ teaspoon celery powder

2 tablespoons Worcestershire sauce

1 tablespoon Louisiana hot sauce

2 teaspoons salt

1 cup dry white wine

For the pâté:

3 tablespoons mayonnaise

1 tablespoon horseradish sauce

1 tablespoon onion powder

2 teaspoons steak sauce

½ teaspoon garlic powder

½ teaspoon dillweed

½ teaspoon salt

¼ teaspoon cayenne pepper

Place the alligator in a large pot and cover with water by one inch and add the seasonings. Bring to a boil and let boil until tender, about 30 minutes. Drain in a colander until nearly dry.

When the alligator has cooled down, put it in a food processor and process until smooth. Add the pâté ingredients and process again until smooth. Chill and serve on crackers, bread, or toast.

Pork Pâté

MAKES 8 TO 10 SERVINGS

3 pounds cooked pork fingers (see page 101)

Pitted olives to taste

1 cup mayonnaise

2 tablespoons olive oil

1 tablespoon Durkee's Famous Sauce

1 tablespoon horseradish sauce

1 tablespoon Louisiana hot sauce

1 teaspoon onion powder

½ teaspoon garlic powder

Put all the ingredients in a food processor and process until smooth. Chill and serve on crackers.

Chicken Pâté

**4 cups shredded cooked chicken
   (dark meat only)**

½ cup dill relish, drained

½ cup mayonnaise

**1 tablespoon Creole or Grey Poupon
   mustard**

1 teaspoon onion powder

½ teaspoon garlic powder

¼ teaspoon cayenne pepper

Put all the ingredients in a food processor and process until smooth. Chill and serve on crackers or toast. Dis tastes even better when it's chilled for a while.

Boiled Pork Fingers

Have you ever seen a hog's finger before? When dis is cooked, you don' have to make a salad or a pâté. You can eat it jus' like it is because it tastes damn' good, I garontee.

MAKES 6 SERVINGS

6 to 8 pork fingers (boneless rib meat)

Salt to taste

2 tablespoons Worcestershire sauce

1 tablespoon Louisiana hot sauce

¾ cup dry white wine

1 teaspoon garlic powder

1 tablespoon onion powder

½ teaspoon dried mint

Combine all the ingredients in a medium-size pot and cover with water by 2 inches. Bring to a boil and continue to boil until the meat is tender and cooked through. Drain and use the meat to make a salad or a pâté, or just eat as is.

Oysters and Link Sausage in Wine

MAKES 8 TO 10 APPETIZER SERVINGS

2 pounds smoked sausage

1½ quarts shucked oysters, drained

2 cups dry white wine

2 teaspoons Louisiana hot sauce

1 teaspoon garlic powder

1 tablespoon soy sauce

Juice from 1 large lemon

Cut the sausage into 1-inch-thick slices and place in a large frying pan, preferably a cast-iron one. Add the oysters, wine, hot sauce, garlic powder, soy sauce, and lemon juice and bring to a good boil. Then turn the fire down very low so that it will cook slowly. Cook until most of the juice is gone, leaving just enough to serve as gravy if you wish. Be sure that sausage is well cooked and tender.

Shrimp Dip

2 pounds peeled boiled shrimp

   (see page 75)

One 8-ounce package cream cheese,

   softened

1 tablespoon fresh lemon juice

1 cup minced green onions

2 to 3 tablespoons mayonnaise, as you like it

1 tablespoon Worcestershire sauce

Salt to taste

1 teaspoon cayenne pepper

Place the shrimp in a food processor and chop. Add the remaining ingredients one at a time to the food processor, processing after each addition.

Egg and Picante Dip

MAKES 4 SERVINGS

3 extra-large or 4 large hard-boiled eggs,
  peeled and chopped
¼ cup mild picante sauce
Salt to taste
1 tablespoon chopped onions

Mix all the ingredients together, then place in a food processor and process until almost smooth.

Eggplant Appetizer

Don't be surprised if you get your hand broken reaching for someone else's eggplant.

3 small eggplant

3 tablespoons olive oil

3 tablespoons sifted all-purpose flour

½ cup chopped fresh parsley

½ cup finely chopped onions

½ cup finely chopped bell peppers

I tablespoon finely chopped garlic

I ½ cups dry red wine

I cup tomato sauce

I tablespoon Worcestershire sauce

I teaspoon cayenne pepper

I ½ teaspoons salt

Up to I cup water, if needed

2 cups grated Romano cheese

Peel the eggplant and cut lengthwise into slices ⅛ to ¼ inch thick. Place the slices in salted water to cover and let them soak for about 2 hours. Rinse and place them in a colander to drain before starting the next step. (While the eggplant is soaking, the rest of the recipe can be prepared.)

Heat the olive oil in a medium-size pot over a medium fire, then add the flour and, stirring constantly, make a roux (see my directions on page 49). When it's as dark as you like, add the parsley, onions, bell peppers, and garlic and cook over a very low fire for 20 to 30 minutes, stirring constantly.

Add the wine, tomato sauce, Worcestershire, cayenne, and salt. Add some water if the sauce is too thick. Cook over a slow fire for about 1 hour.

Heat enough olive oil to cover the bottom of a large frying pan and fry the drained eggplant slices to a deep brown on both sides. Place some of the slices on a platter and sprinkle with some of the Romano cheese. Then spread the sauce freely over the slices. Continue to layer the eggplant, cheese, and sauce until all used up. This can be served hot, or you may chill it in the refrigerator, then slice it like fudge and serve cold. Many prefer this way of serving.

Boiled Burr Artichokes

MAKES 4 TO 8 SERVINGS, DEPENDING ON HOW

ARTICHOKE-HUNGRY YOU ARE

4 fresh artichokes

½ cup olive oil

I cup chopped onions

½ cup fresh lemon juice

I tablespoon chopped garlic

I cup dry white wine

2 teaspoons Louisiana hot sauce

I tablespoon Worcestershire sauce

Salt to taste

Wash the artichokes well and let them drain. Place them in a pot just large enough for the liquids to cover them, or nearly so. Pour the olive oil over them, then put in the onions, lemon juice, and garlic. Pour in the wine and add the hot sauce and Worcestershire. Add enough water just to cover the artichokes. Season with salt. Cook, covered, over a medium fire, adding additional water as needed. It is not necessary, however, to keep the artichokes covered with liquid when they near completion of cooking. Cook until the outside leaves are very tender. When the artichokes are done, remove them from the heat but keep them covered so they will steam for about 30 minutes. Drain, then let cool or chill and serve.

Justin Wilson's Easy Cookin'

Garlic Bread and Wine

**6 tablespoons (¾ stick) margarine or butter,
   softened**

1 tablespoon garlic powder

Grated Romano cheese to taste

Cayenne pepper to taste

1 loaf French bread

Red dinner wine

Cream the margarine with the garlic powder. Beat in the Romano cheese, making sure the mixture spreads easily. Sprinkle with the cayenne.

Slice the French bread lengthwise and then cut into slices. Spread the garlic mixture on generously. Toast in the oven under the broiler.

Dunk the garlic bread in wine when eating it. "Dunk" means "dip." I don't mean sop–sopping is not dunking. Sopping is when you sop the last bit of gravy on your plate with your bread.

Salads, Soups, and Stews

Salads and soups help make any meal good or better.

I love both of dem. Now stews can be an entrée,

and I love to make dem.

Elbow Macaroni Salad

For the salad:

1 pound elbow macaroni

1 cup finely chopped onions

2 cups dill pickles, drained and finely
   chopped

1 cup finely chopped green onions

1 cup finely chopped celery

1 cup finely chopped fresh parsley
   (stems and leaves)

1 cup pimiento-stuffed olives, drained and
   finely chopped

½ cup finely chopped bell peppers

1 cup grated cheddar cheese

2 cups finely chopped hard-boiled eggs

For the dressing:

1 cup mayonnaise, or as much as you like

¼ cup Creole mustard

Louisiana hot sauce or cayenne pepper to
   taste

2 tablespoons olive oil

2 tablespoons fresh lemon juice

Salt to taste

Cook the macaroni according to the
package directions, drain, and cool.
Combine in a large mixing bowl with
the rest of the salad ingredients.

Whisk together the dressing ingredients
and blend this into the salad ingredients.
If it is still too dry, add more mayonnaise.
Refrigerate for 1 day before serving.

Hot Cabbage Slaw

MAKES 8 TO 10 SERVINGS

4 strips thick-sliced bacon, cut into small
   pieces
1 cup chopped onions
½ cup chopped fresh parsley
1 cup chopped bell peppers
1 medium-size head cabbage, shredded
Two 15- or 16-ounce cans whole tomatoes or
   2 pounds fresh tomatoes if you have
   them, cut up
1 teaspoon cayenne pepper
Salt to taste
1 tablespoon red wine vinegar (optional)

Fry the bacon in a large frying pan. Add the onions, parsley, and bell peppers and cook over a medium fire, stirring, until the onions are clear. Add the cabbage and mix well. Add the tomatoes, cayenne, and salt and let simmer for 45 minutes. (Some like to add the vinegar for tartness.) Serve hot.

Country Egg Salad

Dis makes a damn' good sandwich. If you are a city slicker, you can use deviled ham instead of potted meat.

MAKES ENOUGH FOR 10 EGG SALAD SANDWICHES

4 jumbo or extra-large hard-boiled eggs, peeled and chopped

¼ cup pimiento-stuffed olives, drained and minced

One 5½-ounce can potted meat

2 teaspoons olive oil

2 tablespoons mayonnaise

2 teaspoons Louisiana hot sauce

¼ teaspoon garlic powder

1 teaspoon onion powder

Mash the eggs real fine (mash with table fork). Add the olives and mix well. Add the rest of the ingredients and mix well. Serve as a salad or sandwich spread.

Egg and Potato Salad

For the salad:

6 cups peeled and mashed boiled potatoes,
    seasoned

1 cup chopped onions

4 large hard-boiled eggs, peeled and chopped

2 cups chopped dill pickles

(Crushed saltine crackers if needed)

For the dressing:

1 cup mayonnaise

2 tablespoons Durkee's Famous Sauce

3 tablespoons olive oil

1 teaspoon garlic powder

1 tablespoon Louisiana hot sauce

Mix together the salad ingredients except the saltines in a large bowl. In a small bowl, beat together the dressing ingredients. Add it to the salad and mix to coat evenly. Add crushed saltines if the salad is too soupy.

Picnic Potato Salad

THIS'LL SERVE A MOB, 15 TO 20 PEOPLE

For the salad:

5 pounds potatoes, peeled, cut up, boiled in
    water to cover until tender, and drained

4 extra large hard-boiled eggs, chopped

1 cup chopped celery

1¼ cups chopped onions

1 cup chopped dill pickles

½ cup chopped sweet pickles

1 cup pimiento-stuffed green olives, drained
    and chopped

1 cup chopped black olives

Salt to taste

For the dressing:

2 tablespoons olive oil

2 cups mayonnaise

2 tablespoons horseradish sauce

3 tablespoons mild picante sauce

Mix all the salad ingredients together real well in a large mixing bowl.

In a medium-size mixing bowl, beat the olive oil into the mayonnaise, then beat in the horseradish. Stir in the picante sauce. Pour the mixture over the salad ingredients and toss until evenly coated.

Salads, Soups, and Stews

Potato Salad Without Potatoes

I've cooked this for a lot of people and no one ever seems to notice it doesn't have potatoes in it.

MAKES 15 TO 20 SERVINGS

4 stay-fresh bags saltine crackers

I cup chopped celery

I cup chopped onions

I cup sweet relish or chopped sweet pickles, drained

I cup dill relish or chopped dill pickles, drained

I tablespoon horseradish sauce

6 large hard-boiled eggs, chopped

Louisiana hot sauce to taste

I tablespoon Worcestershire sauce

I cup pimiento-stuffed olives, drained and chopped, or as much as you like

I cup pitted black olives, drained and chopped

I cup chopped green onions

Enough mayonnaise to achieve the consistency you like

Crumble the crackers and mix together well with all the other ingredients in a large mixing bowl. If you serve the next day, you might have to add more mayonnaise because the crackers drink up all those tasty juices.

Chicken Salad

To cook the chicken:

10 chicken wings, fat removed

10 chicken thighs, fat removed

1 cup dry white wine

Salt and cayenne pepper to taste

1 tablespoon steak sauce

2 teaspoons garlic powder

2 tablespoons onion powder

1 teaspoon dried mint

1 cup dried parsley

For the salad:

1 cup pimiento-stuffed olives, drained and
  ground in the food processor

¾ cup chopped onions, ground in the food
  processor

1 cup chopped celery, ground in the food
  processor

For the dressing:

1 cup mayonnaise

1 tablespoon Durkee's Famous Sauce

2 tablespoons olive oil

2 tablespoons mild picante sauce

½ teaspoon garlic powder

1 teaspoon salt

Place all the chicken ingredients in a large pot, cover with water, and bring to a boil. Continue to boil until the chicken is very tender. Remove the chicken from the stock. (Save the stock for consommé or gumbo.) Let the chicken cool, then remove the meat from the bones and grind it in a food processor.

Combine the chicken and other salad ingredients in a large mixing bowl and set aside.

Combine the mayonnaise, Durkee's, and olive oil in a small mixing bowl. With a whisk, beat until it returns to the consistency of mayonnaise. Add the picante sauce, garlic powder, and salt and mix well. Stir into the chicken mixture until well combined.

Chicken Salad Without Chicken

MAKES 6 TO 8 SERVINGS

1 beef tongue, boiled in water to cover until tender, peeled, and finely chopped in the food processor

1 cup finely chopped celery

1 cup finely chopped fresh parsley

½ cup pimiento-stuffed olives, drained and finely chopped

½ cup dill relish, drained

½ cup sweet relish, drained

1 cup mayonnaise

¾ cup finely chopped onions

2 teaspoons Louisiana hot sauce

1 tablespoon steak sauce

Salt to taste

Place all the ingredients in a large mixing bowl and combine well.

Beef Salad or Pâté

If you're making a salad, don' use the food processor. If you're making a pâté, throw everything in the food processor and process until smooth.

1½ pounds boneless beef (brisket or any other inexpensive cut), boiled in seasoned water to cover until tender and ground in a food processor

2 cups pimiento-stuffed olives, drained

¼ cup dill relish, drained

2 tablespoons horseradish sauce

2½ teaspoons Louisiana hot sauce

2 tablespoons Worcestershire sauce

6 heaping tablespoons mayonnaise (or less; depends on how juicy it gets)

Salt to taste

Mix everything together until thoroughly combined.

Ham Salad

¼ cup mayonnaise

2 tablespoons olive oil

1 tablespoon Worcestershire sauce

1 tablespoon Durkee's Famous Sauce

Salt to taste

Louisiana hot sauce to taste

1 pound ham, ground in a food processor

3 tablespoons dill relish, drained

2 cups chopped purple onions or regular
  onions if you can't find purple

Make the dressing by combining the mayonnaise with the olive oil and beating it back to its original consistency. Add the Worcestershire and Durkee's and beat to combine, then season with salt and hot sauce. Mix in the ham, dill relish, and onions and combine thoroughly.

Ham Salad II

4 cups chopped ham, ground in a food
    processor

¾ to 1 cup mayonnaise, as you like it

1 tablespoon Creole mustard

2 tablespoons dill relish, drained

2 tablespoons sweet relish, drained

2 teaspoons Louisiana hot sauce

1 tablespoon steak sauce

Mix all the ingredients together real well. Usually no salt is needed.

Minced Ham and Egg Salad

MAKES 10 TO 12 SERVINGS

6 large hard-boiled eggs, chopped

2 pounds ham, chopped

Salt to taste

¼ cup mayonnaise, or as much as you like

1 tablespoon picante sauce

1 tablespoon dill relish, drained, or as much as you like

1½ cups pimiento-stuffed olives, drained and chopped

Combine the eggs and ham in a large mixing bowl and season with salt. Add the remaining ingredients and mix thoroughly.

Fish Salad

MAKES 4 TO 6 SERVINGS

4 cups flaked cooked fish filets (left over fish
  is best)

3 large hard-boiled eggs, chopped

2 to 3 tablespoons mayonnaise, as you like it

Creole mustard to taste

Louisiana hot sauce or cayenne pepper to
  taste

½ cup chopped onions

½ cup dill relish, drained

Salt to taste

Put all the ingredients in a food processor and process until almost smooth. Serve over lettuce.

Avocado Dressing

2 ripe avocados

3 tablespoons red wine vinegar

3 tablespoons mayonnaise

3 tablespoons olive oil

1 tablespoon soy sauce

½ teaspoon cayenne pepper

Peel the avocados, cut in half, pit, and mash the avocado meat well. Pour a little of the vinegar over the avocados to keep them from turning brown. Mix together with the other ingredients, stirring after each addition. Serve over a mixed green salad. If it does not pour easily enough, add more mayonnaise.

Dressing for Green Salad

MAKES 2½ CUPS

2 cups mayonnaise

2 tablespoons garlic powder

3 tablespoons onion powder

1 tablespoon Louisiana hot sauce

2 tablespoons red wine vinegar

2 teaspoons dillweed

1 tablespoon Worcestershire sauce

Mix together all the ingredients until smooth. Pour over a green salad. (Dressing will keep covered for up to 1 month in the refrigerator.)

Coleslaw Dressing

MAKES 2 CUPS

1½ cups mayonnaise

3 tablespoons Durkee's Famous Sauce

1 tablespoon horseradish sauce

2 tablespoons olive oil

¼ cup fresh lemon juice

1 tablespoon garlic powder

Salt to taste

1 tablespoon Louisiana hot sauce or cayenne
    pepper, or as much as you like

1 tablespoon Worcestershire sauce

Mix together the mayonnaise, Durkee's, and horseradish. Add the olive oil and beat until the original consistency of the mayonnaise returns. Add the garlic powder and salt and mix well. Add the hot sauce and Worcestershire and mix well. Add the lemon juice and mix real well.

Add to slaw and toss to coat evenly.

Fish Scraps Courtbouillon

MAKES 6 TO 8 SERVINGS

1 cup dried onions

½ cup dried bell peppers

1 cup chopped green onions

1 teaspoon garlic powder

1 cup dried parsley

1 teaspoon dried mint

1 cup dry white wine

1 tablespoon Worcestershire sauce

2 teaspoons salt

2 teaspoons Louisiana hot sauce

3 to 5 pounds scraps of fish (not the entrails)
   left over from fileting

Cook all of the ingredients except the fish together in a medium-size pot with water to cover until the veggies are rehydrated. Add the fish and bring to a boil. Simmer for 1 hour. *Do not stir after the fish is added;* as the courtbouillon cooks, the bones will drop to the bottom. Once it is done, carefully pour off the courtbouillon, leaving the bones and other solids behind in the pot.

Dumplings and Fish Courtbouillon

MAKES 6 TO 8 SERVINGS

3 tablespoons olive oil

½ cup all-purpose flour

3 cups chopped green onions

½ cup chopped bell peppers

2 cups chopped fresh parsley

½ cup chopped celery

2 teaspoons chopped garlic

10 cups water

2 cups thinly sliced carrots

I cup dry white wine

I teaspoon dried mint

I teaspoon cayenne pepper

2 tablespoons Worcestershire sauce

Salt to taste

4 pounds freshwater fish filets (I like bass and
    catfish)

For the dumplings:

2 cups all-purpose flour

2¼ teaspoons baking powder

¼ teaspoon cayenne pepper

I teaspoon salt

I teaspoon baking soda (only if using
    buttermilk)

1⅓ cups milk or buttermilk

Heat the olive oil in a large pot over a medium fire, then add the flour and, stirring constantly, make a roux (see my directions on page 49). When the roux is medium brown, add the chopped ingredients. Slowly add 2 cups of the water, stirring all the while. Slowly stir in another 2 cups of the water, making sure no lumps form. Pour in the remaining 6 cups water and stir. Add the carrots, wine, mint, Worcestershire, and salt and let cook, stirring occasionally, until the carrots are tender, at least 30 minutes. Add the fish and cook for about 5 minutes.

Meanwhile, to make the dumplings, combine the flour, baking powder, cayenne, and salt in a large mixing bowl (if you use buttermilk, also add the baking soda). Add the milk and stir until the flour is all wet; don't stir too much.

Turn up the heat under the courtbouillon so that it boils. Drop the batter by spoonfuls into the mixture, cover, and cook for 20 minutes.

Fish Bisque

I read dis recipe and got hungry right quick.

MAKES 10 SERVINGS

2 pounds freshwater fish filets, ground in a
food processor

1½ cups chopped onions

1 cup chopped green onions

Chopped fresh parsley to taste

1½ teaspoons chopped garlic

4 large eggs

Salt to taste

Louisiana hot sauce to taste

2 cups seasoned bread crumbs

Fish Stew (recipe follows)

Preheat the oven to 350 degrees. In a large bowl, mix together the fish, onions, green onions, parsley, and garlic. In a small bowl, beat the eggs together with the salt and hot sauce, then mix in with the ground fish. Add the bread crumbs and mix well.

Form into a loaf in the bottom of a large oiled casserole dish and bake for 20 minutes. Then pour the stew around and over the loaf, cover, and bake for another hour. Serve the stew over cooked rice with a slice of the loaf.

Fish Stew

Dis is a stew that you use for many t'ings. When you make a fish bisque, you use it. Or if you would like a fish stew with rice, you could use it. Or if you just want to pour it over toast. Man, that is good stuff, I garontee!

MAKES 10 SERVINGS

¾ cup olive oil

1½ to 2 cups sifted all-purpose flour

2 cups chopped onions

1 cup chopped fresh parsley

6 cups fish stock or water

2 teaspoons chopped garlic

2 tablespoons steak sauce

Louisiana hot sauce to taste

Salt to taste

1 cup dry white wine

3 to 5 pounds fish filets, cut into chunks

In a large pot, heat the oil over a medium fire, then add the flour and make a thick, dark roux (see my directions on page 49). After the roux has darkened, stir in the onions and parsley; continue cooking and stirring until the onions are clear. Add 2 cups of the stock to the roux and stir until a thick paste has formed. Stir in the garlic, steak sauce, hot sauce, salt, and wine until well blended. Stirring, add the remaining 4 cups stock and the fish. Reduce the fire to low, cover, and let simmer for 45 minutes. Serve over cooked rice.

How to Make a Roux

Roux is the foundation of many Cajun dishes. You will find it referred to in a number of the recipes in this book. The roux that follows is the one I have used for many years, with great success—I garontee!

1½ cups oil or bacon drippings

1½ cups sifted all-purpose flour

Heat the oil in a large, heavy pot over a medium fire. Add the flour and cook very slowly, stirring almost constantly. The flour must be cooked to a very dark brown, nearly black but not actually burned. This takes more time than you might think is necessary, but a good roux must be cooked slowly to get the floury taste out of it and to ensure uniformity of color. This is the basic roux. Cajuns will say that a finished roux shines.

Although all roux are pretty much the same in Cajun kitchens, there are variations practiced by some stubborn ol' cooks. For instance, after you have made the basic roux, you can add a small can of tomato paste, stirring this all the time until the roux returns to the color of the flour before the paste was added. Then add a small can of tomato sauce, stirring this into the mixture until it turns dark brown again.

Oyster Soup

MAKES 4 SERVINGS

2 cups oyster juice

8 cups water

1 cup chopped onions

1 cup chopped green onions

1 tablespoon chopped bell peppers

2 tablespoons Worcestershire sauce

1 tablespoon Louisiana hot sauce

1 tablespoon salt

1 teaspoon dried mint

2 dozen shucked oysters

Put all the ingredients except the oysters in a large pot and cook for 30 to 40 minutes at a nice simmer. Add the oysters, cook for another 15 minutes, and serve.

Turtle Soup

Dis a delicious soup and I had a hard time getting dis recipe together. But dat is a long story and I can't talk about dat right now.

MAKES 12 SERVINGS

3 tablespoons olive oil

1 cup sifted all-purpose flour

1 cup finely chopped green onions

½ cup finely chopped fresh parsley

2 quarts turtle stock (see page 53) or chicken stock

1 cup tomato sauce

4 large hard-boiled eggs, finely chopped

½ cup finely chopped lemon with the peel

½ teaspoon cayenne pepper

Salt to taste

2 pounds cleaned turtle meat, cut into ½-inch cubes

Sherry wine to taste

Heat the olive oil in a large pot over a medium fire, then add the flour and, stirring constantly, make a dark roux (see my directions on page 49). Add the green onions and parsley and cook, stirring, until the onions are clear. Stir in the stock, tomato sauce, eggs, and lemon, then season with the cayenne and salt. Keep at a simmer while you brown the turtle meat.

Brown the turtle meat in a large skillet, then add to the stock and cook over a low fire for at least 2 hours, covered.

When you serve, add sherry wine to taste, not more than 1 tablespoon per bowl.

Turtle Stew I

Y ou notice in dis turtle stew I got potato. Dat is because I had to make dis stew for my friend Junior Monteleone. He said he wanted potatoes and he got 'em.

MAKES 12 SERVINGS

1 cup olive oil

2½ cups sifted all-purpose flour

3 cups chopped onions

1 cup chopped bell peppers

1 cup chopped green onions

1 cup chopped fresh parsley

1½ tablespoons chopped garlic

8 to 10 cups cold water (depending on the thickness of the roux)

1 quart turtle stock
   (see Turtle Stew II)

1½ tablespoons fresh lemon juice

2 to 3 tablespoons soy sauce, as you like it

1½ cups dry white wine

Cayenne pepper to taste

1 teaspoon dried mint

4 to 5 pounds cleaned turtle meat, cut up and parboiled in water to cover for 35 to 40 minutes; save the stock

8 medium-size Irish potatoes, peeled and chopped or cut into curlicues

Salt to taste

Heat the oil in a large pot over a medium fire, then add the flour and, stirring constantly, make a dark roux (see my directions on page 49). When brown enough, add the onions and bell peppers and cook, stirring, until the onions are clear. Add the green onions, parsley, and garlic and cook, stirring, for 10 to 15 minutes.

Add 1 cup of the cold water a little at a time, stirring, so that roux will be smooth. Add the rest of the water and the turtle stock. Add the lemon juice, soy sauce, wine, cayenne pepper, and mint, then add the turtle meat, potatoes, and salt. Bring to a boil, then reduce the fire to low, cover, and cook for 3 to 4 hours.

Justin Wilson's Easy Cookin'

Turtle Stew II

Dis the original turtle stew.

MAKES 6 TO 8 SERVINGS

½ cup olive or peanut oil or bacon drippings

1 cup sifted all-purpose flour

2 cups finely chopped onions

½ cup chopped bell peppers

1 cup chopped fresh parsley

1 tablespoon chopped garlic

2 pounds cleaned turtle meat, cut up and parboiled in water to cover for 35 to 40 minutes

½ teaspoon dried mint

2 tablespoons Worcestershire sauce

1 tablespoon Louisiana hot sauce or ½ teaspoon cayenne pepper

Salt to taste

1 cup dry white wine

6 to 10 cups water

Heat the oil in a large pot over a medium fire, then add the flour and, stirring constantly, make a dark roux (see my directions on page 49). Add the onions, bell peppers, parsley, and garlic and cook, stirring, until softened. Add the remaining ingredients, including enough water to get the consistency you like, stir to combine, cover, and cook over a medium-low fire until the meat is tender, about 2 hours.

Corn and Tomato Soup

Dis can make anyone look like a gourmet cook.

MAKES 8 SERVINGS

Two 15½-ounce cans tomato juice

One 15-ounce can whole-kernel corn,
    drained and pureed

One 15-ounce can cream-style corn

1 cup dry red wine (I like to use Chianti
    for this)

2 tablespoons soy sauce

One 10-ounce can Rotel spiced tomatoes,
    processed to a liquid

2 teaspoons Louisiana hot sauce

4 cups water

1 tablespoon onion powder

1 teaspoon garlic powder

Salt if needed

Mix all the ingredients together in a large pot and bring to a boil. Cook over a low fire for 1 hour, stirring occasionally.

Very Low Fat Lentil Soup

For the seasoned stock:

10 to 12 chicken wings

Garlic powder to taste

Onion powder to taste

Dried mint to taste

Salt and cayenne pepper to taste

Dried parsley to taste

For the lentils:

½ pound pickled pork shoulder, parboiled in water to cover until tender, fat removed, and cut into small pieces

1 cup dry white wine

1 pound dried lentils, washed real well

Put all the stock ingredients in a large pot and cover with water. Cook until the chicken is tender and completely cooked. Remove the chicken and use for another dish. Let the stock cool, skim off the fat, and let sit in the refrigerator overnight.

Place the pickled pork in a large pot, pour seasoned stock over it to cover, and bring to a rolling boil. Add the wine and lentils and bring back to a boil. Reduce the fire to low and cook until the lentils are tender.

Red Bean Soup

MAKES 6 TO 8 SERVINGS

I pound dried red beans, washed real well

I cup dry white wine

Onion powder to taste

Garlic powder to taste

Salt to taste

Chopped green onions to taste

Place the beans in a large mixing bowl, cover generously with water, and let soak overnight. Drain.

Put the beans in a medium-size pot, add the wine and water to cover, and bring to a boil. Reduce the fire to medium-low, cover, and cook until the beans mash easily, adding more water if you need to. Season with onion and garlic powder.

Put the cooked beans in a food processor, add salt if necessary, and process to make a nice, thick soup, adding enough water to get the right consistency. Reheat if necessary. Add the green onions to the soup when serving.

Vegetable Soup with Brisket

If you don't eat all dis today, eat the rest tomorrow.

MAKES 10 SERVINGS

1½ pounds beef brisket, fat removed and cut up into small pieces

2 cups Brussels sprouts

½ cup chopped fresh parsley

1 teaspoon dried mint

1½ cups coarsely chopped green onions

1½ cups coarsely chopped onions

1½ cups fresh green snap beans

1 cup coarsely chopped celery

½ cup sweet corn cut and scraped off the cob

1½ cups coarsely chopped fresh tomatoes

2 cups coarsely chopped bell peppers

3 cups peeled and chopped turnips

3½ cups peeled and chopped Irish potatoes

1½ cups dry white wine

2 tablespoons Louisiana hot sauce

4 quarts water

1 tablespoon soy sauce

1 tablespoon finely chopped garlic

Salt to taste

Put all the ingredients in a large pot. Place the lid on the pot and cook over a medium fire until it comes to a boil. Reduce the fire to medium-low and simmer until the brisket is tender, about 2 hours.

Salads, Soups, and Stews

Cold Chicken Consommé

Dis is very good and now you can find out where consommé comes from.

Salt to taste

12 chicken wings, fat removed

10 chicken thighs, fat removed

1 tablespoon steak sauce

1 cup dry white wine

1 tablespoon garlic powder

2 tablespoons onion powder

1 teaspoon dried mint

¾ cup dried parsley

Cayenne pepper to taste

Place all the ingredients in a large pot and add enough water to cover. Bring to a boil and continue to boil until the chicken meat is nearly falling off the bones. Let cool, then take the chicken out of the pot, and place the consommé in the refrigerator overnight. Skim the fat off the consommé. Use the chicken for another dish and serve the consommé, cold or hot, with crackers.

Smoked Pork Backbone Stock

MAKES 4 SERVINGS

6 to 8 large smoked pork backbones

2 tablespoons onion powder

1 tablespoon garlic powder

Louisiana hot sauce to taste

1½ tablespoons Worcestershire sauce

Place everything in a large pot and add enough water to cover. Cook, covered, for about 1 hour. Let cool and skim the fat off the top.

Take the backbone out of the stock and pick the meat out—it makes good eating. Use the stock to cook beans and for making soup.

Chopped Pork and Turnip Stew

MAKES 10 TO 14 SERVINGS

1 cup olive oil

2 cups sifted all-purpose flour

3 cups chopped onions

1 cup chopped celery

1 cup chopped bell peppers

1 cup chopped fresh parsley

2 cups dry white wine

1 teaspoon dried mint

1½ teaspoons minced garlic

2 tablespoons Worcestershire sauce

1 tablespoon Louisiana hot sauce

5 pounds pork fingers (boneless rib meat),
   cut into large pieces

3 to 10 cups peeled and cubed turnips, as you
   like it

Salt to taste

Heat the oil in a large frying pan over a medium fire, then add the flour and, stirring constantly, make a roux (see my directions on page 49). When the roux is as brown as you like, add the onions, celery, bell peppers, and parsley and cook, stirring, until the onions are clear. Add enough cold water to the mixture to get a nice stew-like consistency and cook, covered, for about 1 hour and 10 minutes over a low fire. Stir in the wine, mint, garlic, Worcestershire, and hot sauce.

Meanwhile, brown the meat in a pot big enough to hold everything—turnips, roux, mixture, and meat. Pour the roux mixture into the pot with the meat, add the turnips and water to cover, and cook, covered, for 2 to 3 hours over a medium-low fire, keeping it bubbly. Season with salt.

Justin Wilson's Easy Cookin'

Leftover Steak, Potatoes, and Mushroom Stew

MAKES 4 TO 6 SERVINGS

1½ cups olive oil

1½ cups sifted all-purpose flour

1 cup chopped onions

½ cup cold water, maybe more

2½ pounds cooked boneless steak, fat removed and cut into 1-inch squares

1 pound potatoes, peeled, cut up, boiled until tender in seasoned water to cover, and drained

½ cup dry light red wine (I like Chianti for this)

Louisiana hot sauce to taste

Worcestershire sauce to taste

1 cup sliced mushrooms

Salt to taste

Creole mustard to taste

Heat the olive oil in a large pot over a medium fire. Add the flour and, stirring constantly, make a dark roux (see my directions on page 49). Add the onions and cook, stirring, until clear, then stir in the water until smooth. Add the remaining ingredients and cook, covered, over a low fire for about 45 minutes, adding more water if needed.

Venison Stew

¾ cup olive oil

1½ cups sifted all-purpose flour

1 cup chopped onions

½ cup chopped bell peppers

½ cup chopped fresh parsley

1 cup chopped green onions

4 to 5 cups cold water

3 pounds boneless venison, fat removed and
   cut up for stew

3 cups peeled and cut up potatoes

Salt to taste

Louisiana hot sauce or cayenne pepper to
   taste

1 teaspoon dried mint

1 cup dry white wine

In a large pot, heat the olive oil over a medium fire, then add the flour and, stirring constantly, make a dark roux (see my directions on page 49). Add the onions, bell peppers, parsley, and green onions and cook, stirring, until the onions are clear. Add 4 cups of water and stir until smooth. Add the remaining ingredients and cook the stew for at least 1 hour, covered, until the potatoes and venison are tender, adding more water if needed to get the consistency you want.

Justin Wilson's Easy Cookin'

Bunny Rabbit Stew
(Not the Easter Bunny)

MAKES 8 TO 10 SERVINGS

1 cup olive oil

2 cups sifted all-purpose flour

3 cups water

3½ cups chopped onions

1 cup chopped celery

2 cups chopped bell peppers

2 cups chopped fresh parsley

2 cups dry red wine

2 tablespoons chopped garlic

2 teaspoons Liquid Smoke

3 tablespoons steak sauce

1 tablespoon Louisiana hot sauce

1 tablespoon salt

1 teaspoon dried mint

One 4½-pound dressed rabbit, cut into
    pieces

4 cups peeled and cubed Irish potatoes

Heat the oil in a deep frying pan over a medium fire, then add the flour and, stirring constantly, make a dark roux (see my directions on page 49). Meanwhile, in a large pot, bring the water to a boil.

Add the onions, celery, bell peppers, and parsley to the roux and cook, stirring frequently, until the onions are clear.

Add the wine, garlic, Liquid Smoke, steak sauce, hot sauce, salt, and mint to the boiling water. Add the roux and mix well. Bring back to a boil and add the rabbit. Bring back to a boil again and add the potatoes. Bring to a boil again, reduce the fire to low, and simmer, covered, for 1½ hours, until the rabbit is tender.

Fish and Shellfish

Fish is very important to anyone's diet, I don't care who dey are. I love broiled fish; as for shellfish, I love oysters, broiled or fried. Shrimp, crawfish, and crab are very good cooked mos' any way you would like to. And dey are also delicious in gumbo, I garontee!

Baked Catfish

Some people way up nort' may not know about catfish, so they can use some other kind of fish. But me, I will rather have the catfish.

MAKES 10 SERVINGS

One 10-pound cleaned catfish

Roughly chopped fresh parsley to taste

Salt and cayenne pepper to taste

1 lemon, sliced

¼ cup fresh lemon juice

¼ cup steak sauce

2 teaspoons onion powder

1 teaspoon garlic powder

½ teaspoon dried mint

1½ cups dry white wine

Place the catfish in an oiled roaster pan and sprinkle the parsley around it. Sprinkle the catfish with salt and cayenne pepper and place the lemon slices over it.

Mix the lemon juice, steak sauce, onion powder, garlic powder, mint, and wine together and pour around the fish. Cover and bake in a preheated 300-degree oven for 1 to 1¼ hours. Serve with the sauce.

Fried Filet Fish

Dese fish filets are fileted twice to make them cook quick. When they float, they are done for true.

For the dredge mixture:

2 cups water

1 cup dry white wine

2 tablespoons fresh lemon juice

For the flour mixture:

3 cups corn flour

2 teaspoons onion powder

1 teaspoon Worcestershire powder

½ teaspoon garlic powder

3 teaspoons salt

1 teaspoon cayenne pepper

To cook:

Peanut oil

For the fish:

5 pounds thin fish filets

Mix the dredge ingredients together well in a bowl. Mix the flour ingredients together on a plate.

Fill a deep fryer three quarters full with peanut oil and heat to 350 degrees. Dip the fish filets in the dredge mixture, then roll in the flour mixture, knocking off any excess. Drop the filets in the hot oil in batches and cook until they float. Remove with a slotted spoon and drain on paper towels.

Fried Oysters

When dese oysters float in de hot oil, dey are done.

Peanut oil

3 dozen shucked oysters

2 cups corn flour

2 teaspoons salt

I teaspoon onion powder

I teaspoon celery powder

½ teaspoon garlic powder

Cayenne pepper to taste

Fill a deep fryer three quarters full with peanut oil and heat to 350 degrees. Drain the oysters and place on paper towels to dry. Combine all the dry ingredients in a bowl and mix well. Dredge the oysters in the dry ingredients, knocking off any excess, and fry in the hot oil a dozen at a time until done. Drain on paper towels.

Oyster-Eggplant Jambalaya

My good friend Maurice Dantin cooked dis and invited me to help him eat it. It was so good I asked if I could put it in my cookbook.

MAKES 6 SERVINGS

2 medium-size eggplants, peeled and cut into cubes

4 teaspoons salt

¼ cup (½ stick) margarine or butter or ¼ cup bacon drippings

3 cups chopped onions

1 cup chopped celery

1 cup chopped green onions

¾ cup chopped fresh parsley

4 cloves garlic, minced

2 cups uncooked long-grain rice

1 quart shucked oysters, with their juices

2 teaspoons fresh thyme leaves

2 tablespoons Worcestershire sauce

¼ teaspoon cayenne pepper

3 cups chicken stock

Boil the eggplant with 2 teaspoons of the salt in enough water to cover until tender, about 15 minutes. Pour into a colander and let drain.

Melt the margarine in a large cast-iron frying pan over a medium fire and cook the onions, celery, green onions, parsley, garlic, and rice, stirring, until the vegetables are tender. Cut up or mash the oysters and add to the frying pan with the oyster juices and eggplant cubes. Add the remaining 2 teaspoons salt, the thyme, Worcestershire, cayenne, and chicken stock and bring to a boil. Cover and cook in a preheated 350-degree oven or on top of the stove over low heat until all the juices are absorbed by the rice, about 45 minutes, stirring occasionally.

Crabmeat Étouffée

Dis is so easy to cook and it tastes so good, you are going to think somebody lied to you about how good it is, I garontee.

MAKES 4 SERVINGS

½ cup (1 stick) margarine or butter

4 cups chopped onions

1 cup chopped green onions

1 cup chopped bell peppers

1½ cups chopped fresh parsley

2 cups dry white wine

1 tablespoon steak sauce

1 teaspoon minced garlic

2 pounds crabmeat, picked over for shells
   and cartilage

Salt to taste

2 tablespoons mild picante sauce

In a large frying pan, melt the margarine over a medium fire. Add the onions, green onions, bell peppers, and parsley and cook, stirring, until the onions are clear. Add the wine, steak sauce, and garlic and cook for 10 minutes more, stirring a couple of times. Add the crabmeat, salt, and picante sauce and stir to mix well. Reduce the heat to low, cover, and simmer for 30 to 45 minutes. Serve over cooked rice or pasta.

Crawfish Étouffée

Dis is more or less the original Cajun recipe for étouffée. And I like it very much jus' like it is.

MAKES 6 SERVINGS

½ cup (1 stick) margarine or butter

6 cups chopped onions (or the same volume measure as the crawfish)

1½ cups chopped green onions

1½ cups chopped fresh parsley

¼ cup fresh lemon juice

2 tablespoons soy sauce

2 teaspoons minced garlic

4 to 5 pounds crawfish tails, peeled

Salt to taste

Louisiana hot sauce or cayenne pepper to taste

In a large frying pan, melt the margarine over a medium fire. Add the onions, green onions, and parsley and cook, stirring, until the onions are clear. Add the lemon juice, soy sauce, and garlic and cook, stirring, for 10 minutes more. Add the crawfish, salt, and hot sauce and stir to mix well. Reduce the fire to low, cover, and simmer for 30 to 45 minutes. Serve over cooked rice or pasta.

Crawfish Mashed Potato Casserole

MAKES 4 TO 6 SERVINGS

To cook the potatoes:

2 tablespoons garlic powder

2 tablespoons onion powder

2 teaspoons salt

Cayenne pepper to taste

10 cups peeled and cut-up potatoes

For the casserole:

½ cup olive oil

3 tablespoons Louisiana hot sauce

1 tablespoon onion powder

1 teaspoon dillweed

½ teaspoon garlic powder

¾ cup dry white wine

2 tablespoons Worcestershire sauce

2 teaspoons salt

2 pounds crawfish tails, peeled

Seasoned bread crumbs

Bring a large pot of water, with the garlic and onion powders, salt, and cayenne, to a boil, then add the potatoes and boil until tender. Drain and mash good.

Mix the potatoes with the remaining ingredients except the bread crumbs, adding them one at a time and stirring after each addition. Place the mixture in a casserole dish and cook in a preheated 325-degree oven for 45 minutes. Sprinkle the bread crumbs over the top of the casserole and serve.

Crawfish Maque Chou

MAKES 4 TO 6 SERVINGS

½ cup olive oil

1 cup chopped onions

¾ cup chopped bell peppers

1 tablespoon dried parsley or 1 cup chopped
    fresh parsley

4 cups corn cut and scraped off the cob or
    canned whole-kernel corn, drained

1 cup dry white wine

1 cup water

1 teaspoon finely chopped garlic

Salt and cayenne pepper to taste

1 tablespoon steak sauce

2 pounds crawfish tails, peeled

Heat the olive oil in a large frying pan over a medium fire, then cook the onions, bell peppers, and parsley, stirring, until the onions are clear and the peppers are cooked. Add the corn and stir real well, then add the wine, water, and garlic. Stir in the salt, cayenne, and steak sauce, reduce the fire to low, cover, and cook until the corn is done, about 20 minutes.

Add the crawfish and bring to a boil. Lower the fire and cook for 10 to 15 minutes.

Boiled Shrimp in the Shell

MAKES 4 TO 6 SERVINGS

3 quarts water (or enough to cover the shrimp)

2 tablespoons cayenne pepper

8 lemons, quartered

3 large onions, quartered

2 cloves garlic, coarsely chopped

One 6-pack nonalcoholic beer

2 tablespoons Worcestershire sauce

Salt to taste

5 pounds shrimp in their shells

Put the water along with the cayenne in a pot large enough to hold the shrimp and place it over a hot fire. Place the lemons, onions, and garlic in the water. Add the beer and Worcestershire. Add salt until the mixture is too salty for your taste. Bring to a boil, then add the shrimp. Cook for 15 to 25 minutes, depending on the size of the shrimp. When their shells stand away from the meat, they are done. Another way to tell is that they usually float when cooked. But the best way to determine whether the shrimp are done is to taste them after 15 to 20 minutes of boiling.

Pour the liquid off the shrimp and let them steam for 15 minutes. Then place on a large tray and cool.

Variation:
Substitute 2 to 3 dozen crabs for the shrimp. Add more salt, since crabs and other shellfish require more than do shrimp.

Boiled Shrimp in the Shell and a 6-Pack of Beer

MAKES 4 TO 6 SERVINGS

3 quarts water (or enough to cover the
   shrimp)

One 6-pack beer

1 cup onion powder

¼ cup garlic powder

¾ cup Worcestershire sauce

5 tablespoons salt

2 teaspoons dried mint

6 large lemons, quartered

5 pounds shrimp in their shells

Combine all the ingredients except the shrimp in a large pot and bring to a boil. Add the shrimp and continue to boil until the shrimp are pink. Drain and serve.

You notice I said cook until the shrimp are pink, but when they float they are done. Us Cajuns like to put a few ice cubes in the water after they are cooked. Dis cools them shrimp down.

Shrimp and Macaroni Casserole

1½ pounds macaroni

4 teaspoons salt

1 tablespoon onion powder

1 teaspoon garlic powder

2 tablespoons olive oil

¼ teaspoon cayenne pepper

2 pounds shrimp, peeled and deveined

2 tablespoons Louisiana hot sauce

One 16-ounce bottle mild picante sauce

Bring a large pot of water to a boil, then add the macaroni, salt, onion and garlic powders, olive oil, and cayenne and boil the macaroni until tender. Drain.

Mix the macaroni, shrimp, hot sauce, and picante sauce together and pour into a casserole dish. Cook in a preheated 350-degree oven for 1 hour.

No-Fat Turtle Sauce Piquant

You always remove the fat from turtle meat, but in this recipe I didn' use any oil at all and I'll be doggone, it tasted good.

MAKES 6 TO 8 SERVINGS, AT LEAST

1½ cups sifted all-purpose flour

3 quarts water

2 cups chopped onions or 1 cup dried onions

1 cup chopped bell peppers or ½ cup dried bell peppers

1 cup chopped green onions or ½ cup dried green onions

1½ cups chopped fresh parsley or ¾ cup dried parsley

1 teaspoon celery powder

2 teaspoons garlic powder

1 teaspoon dried mint

4 cups tomato sauce

3 tablespoons Worcestershire sauce

2 tablespoons Louisiana hot sauce or 1 teaspoon cayenne pepper

2½ to 3 pounds cleaned turtle meat, cut up

Make a dry roux by browning the flour in a large pot on top of the stove or in a preheated 400-degree oven, stirring frequently either way.

Add half of the water to the flour, mixing well. Stir in the remaining water, then add the remaining ingredients except the turtle meat and cook until the veggies are softened. Add the turtle meat and bring to a boil. Reduce the fire to low, cover, and cook for 2 hours. Serve this over cooked rice.

Poultry, Meat, and Game

Poultry—that's chicken, turkey, duck, and goose. Chicken can make a fine meal broiled, fried, baked, or barbecued. My favorite way of cooking turkey is to deep-fry it whole. As far as meats are concerned, I like them all, beef, lamb, and pork. You can cook them many different ways and make a good, good, easy meal.

Venison is fine game. Quail and doves taste wonderful. Elk and antelope are delicious (though I don't have any recipes for either of them—you'll just have to make your own up).

Baked Chicken

MAKES 4 TO 6 SERVINGS

Salt and cayenne pepper

1 large hen

Dressing of your choice, if you like

2 cups chicken stock

Rub salt and cayenne pepper into the hen, then place it on a rack in a roaster pan. Stuff with the dressing, pour the stock around the hen, and bake in a preheated 350-degree oven until tender and done, 1½ to 2 hours, depending on the size of the hen.

Baked Broiled Chicken

MAKES 4 SERVINGS

Olive oil

4 chicken halves

3 tablespoons steak sauce

3 large cloves garlic, peeled

I cup dry white wine

I cup water

I teaspoon dried mint

½ cup dried parsley

I medium-size onion, quartered

3 cups ground walnuts

Preheat the broiler. Grease a large broiler pan with olive oil and place the chicken halves in the pan, then broil until almost cooked through.

While the chickens are broiling, mix together the remaining ingredients except the walnuts. When the chickens are about done, sprinkle the walnuts over them, then the wine mixture. Turn the oven temperature down to 300 degrees and cook until the chickens are cooked all the way through, basting often.

Chicken à la Creole

Dis Chicken à la Creole is fixed dis easy way to help people who don' have time to cook, which mos' people like to do, including me.

¼ cup dried onions

1 tablespoon dried green onions

1 tablespoon dried parsley

1 teaspoon garlic powder

4 cups water or chicken stock

1 cup dry white wine

1 cup Rotel spiced tomatoes

3 tablespoons steak sauce

1 to 2 teaspoons Louisiana hot sauce or
   ½ teaspoon cayenne pepper, as you like it

4 cups canned peeled tomatoes

4 cups boneless boiled chicken pieces, from a
   chicken boiled in water to cover

1 teaspoon dried mint

Mix the onions, green onions, parsley, and garlic powder with 2 cups of the water and set aside. Let this mixture soak for about 1 hour.

Meanwhile, combine the remaining 2 cups water, the wine, tomatoes, steak sauce, hot sauce, and peeled tomatoes in a large pot and cook for about 30 minutes over a low fire.

Add the rehydrated vegetables and liquid to the pot and stir well. Add the chicken and mint and stir well. Place the lid on the pot and cook over a low to medium-low fire for 1 to 1½ hours. Serve over cooked rice.

Chicken Casserole

Dis looks like a hard recipe, but it's not, no. Jus' follow the instructions that's on there an' it will come out good, I garontee.

MAKES 12 SERVINGS

6 large eggs, well beaten

1 cup dry white wine

2 tablespoons Louisiana hot sauce

½ cup water

8 cups cooked macaroni

1 cup pecans, boiled in water to cover with
    ½ teaspoon salt until tender (save the
    cooking water to use as stock for other
    dishes)

6 cups shredded cooked chicken, from
    chicken boiled in seasoned water to cover

4 cups grated cheddar cheese

½ cup grated Parmesan or Romano cheese

Salt to taste

Seasoned bread crumbs

In a medium-size bowl beat together the eggs, wine, and hot sauce and pour into an oiled casserole dish. Rinse the bowl with the water and pour that into the dish also. Add the other ingredients except the bread crumbs and mix well. Sprinkle the bread crumbs on top and bake in a preheated 325-degree oven for 1 hour and 15 minutes.

Chicken Casserole with Wild Rice

Dis rice isn't all that wild, no, but it is a delicious rice.

MAKES 8 SERVINGS

2 cups cubed cooked chicken, from thighs boiled in seasoned water to cover

2 cups cooked wild rice, seasoned with salt, cayenne pepper, garlic powder, and onion powder to taste

2 cups grated cheddar cheese

I cup steak sauce

2 tablespoons olive oil

Sliced cheddar cheese to cover casserole

Preheat the oven to 350 degrees. Combine all the ingredients in a bowl except the oil and sliced cheese. Grease a casserole dish with the olive oil, then pour in the mixture. Place the sliced cheese on top and bake for 30 minutes.

Boiled Chicken Gizzards

MAKES 3 TO 4 SERVINGS

½ teaspoon garlic powder

1 teaspoon onion powder

Salt and cayenne pepper to taste

1 cup dry white wine

1 tablespoon Worcestershire sauce

2 cups water

1 pound chicken gizzards

Place all the ingredients in a saucepan large enough to hold them comfortably. Cover, bring to a boil, and let boil until the gizzards are tender, then drain and serve.

Justin Wilson's Easy Cookin'

Dis is Junior Monteleone. He's watchin' me taste real good food, I garontee! Dis was cooked on a Cajun microwave.

Dis is Doris Monteleone watching me take a delicious piece of meat from my big smoker-cooker barbecue pit.

Dis is a wild turkey
dat we caught and
deep-fried.

Dis is a beef brisket dat we deep-fried jus' to see how it would turn out. And it turned out good. Oooh boy!

Dis is my friend Walter Guitreau showing off a beef brisket dat we cooked in my smoker-cooker barbecue pit.

Me and my good friend Maurice Dantin are checking out some barbecued meat dat tasted real good.

Dese little slender fellows, Junior Monteleone in the center and Charlie Blackwell on the left, are in front of my smoker-cooker barbecue pit dat has a **P-I-G** hog cookin' in it. And dat is me on the right.

Dis is Doris and Junior Monteleone in front of the oven they bake real-good-tastin' bread in.

Here is some bread out of dat beautemous oven. Me and my secretary, Jackie McKenzie, love to eat de bread Junior and Doris bake. It is good, I garontee!

Here is Jackie, helping me do a cooking show in Macon, Georgia. And she did a very fine job, she did.

Dis is a good picture of de Cajun microwave.

I am basting briskets with my basting sauce in my big smoker-cooker microwave pit.

Dis is a picture of me with **Mr.** and **Mrs. Robert Ricks.** I am showing dem how to stuff dis pig right.

Dis pasta salad is more different than any you ever tasted. But it is good, ooooh boy.

I wont you to cast your eye on dis. Dis is shrimp boiled the Cajun way. I garontee.

Dis a picture of my daughter, Sara, and her husband, Bob, and me. Sara helped me do my television show and I sure did need her help, ooooh boy.

Dis is crawfish maque chou. You don' know what dat means, but it tastes real good.

Dis is my good friend **Dr. Charlie Johnson**. He usually helps me cook but he was so busy doctoring, all he had time to do was to come and eat. And by the way he has a wondermous appetite yeah.

You are not going to believe dat dis roast weighed twenty-two pounds. It was a beef roast and we ate every bit of it too.

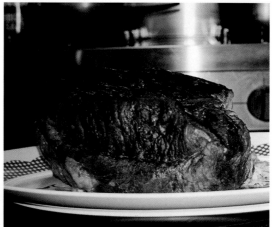

Dis is boiled crawfish and you can do mos' anything you wont with dis. You can eat dem like they are or put them in something else.

Dis is **P-I-G** hog jambalaya. And it tastes so goooood.

Jus' mixing a little pasta salad.

This photo was took while cooking recipes from the cooking show, *Justin Wilson's Easy Cookin'*.
Jim Moriarty is to my left, Dave Landry is behind me, and Paul Combel is to my right.
All dem are television peoples.

My daughter, Sara, is the tall one and the other pretty lady is my secretary, Jackie, who helped me with the cookbook and the cooking show.

Seven Steaks Étouffée

Dis is an easy recipe. Jus' do it like it says and it will be good, I garontee.

MAKES 10 SERVINGS

2 tablespoons olive oil

About 4 pounds seven steaks
    (shoulder steaks)

Salt to taste

2 cups chopped onions

1 cup chopped bell peppers

2 cups chopped mushrooms

1 cup dry white wine

½ cup pimiento-stuffed olives, drained

1 tablespoon chopped garlic

2 tablespoons dried parsley

½ teaspoon celery seed

1 teaspoon dried mint

2 tablespoons steak sauce

2 teaspoons Louisiana hot sauce

Over a medium to high fire, heat the olive oil in a large pot, then brown the steaks on both sides. Season with salt, then add the remaining ingredients. Stir well, then reduce the fire to low and place the lid on the pot. Simmer for 2 to 3 hours. Serve over cooked rice.

Barbecued Beef Roast in a Pan

MAKES 15 TO 20 SERVINGS

One 20-pound beef round roast

10 nice green onions

10 medium-size cloves garlic, peeled

10 hot green peppers (cayenne or jalapeño)

Salt and cayenne pepper to taste

Peanut oil

3 cups dry white wine

Start a fire in a covered barbecue pit, using charcoal (if you can get it), briquettes if you have to. Have the fire lit for 30 minutes before the roast is placed in it, then keep a slow fire going by adding wet pecan wood and charcoal when needed.

While the fire is getting ready, puncture ten deep holes in the roast with a small knife. Push a green onion, a clove of garlic, and a hot pepper into each of the holes. Pat the sides of the roast with salt and cayenne, then place it in a large roaster pan greased with peanut oil. Put the pan on the barbecue fire. Sear all sides of the roast; when seared, pour the wine into the pan, around, not on, the roast. Cook for about 8 hours on a slow fire. Baste the meat frequently and turn it often. If the fire blazes up, sprinkle a little water on it. However, if indirect heat is used, you should not have a problem. If any additional liquid is needed, mix wine and water together in a one-to-one ratio and add to the pan.

Barbecued Brisket

MAKES 12 SERVINGS

One 6-pound brisket

Salt and cayenne pepper to taste

For the basting sauce:

2 cups dry red or white wine

2 cups water

2 tablespoons fresh lemon juice

Garlic powder to taste

A little Louisiana hot sauce

Rub the brisket with salt and cayenne. Combine the basting ingredients. Place the brisket in a smoker stoked with pecan wood, preferably, and smoke over a low fire (250 degrees) overnight or at least 8 hours, basting frequently with the sauce.

Baked Brisket with Potatoes and Carrots

One 4- to 5-pound brisket

Salt and cayenne pepper to taste

6 to 8 potatoes, peeled and cut in half

Cut-up carrots, as many as you want

½ bell pepper, chopped

1 cup chopped fresh parsley

2 cups chopped green onions

2 teaspoons chopped garlic

2 cups water

1 cup dry white wine

2 tablespoons Worcestershire sauce

Rub the meat with salt and cayenne. Place the brisket in a large covered roaster pan. Place the potatoes, carrots, bell pepper, parsley, green onions, and garlic around, not on, the meat. Season the vegetables with salt, pour in the water, wine, and Worcestershire, cover, and cook in a preheated 350-degree oven for 2 hours.

Baked Beef Brisket

MAKES 4 TO 6 SERVINGS

Salt and cayenne pepper to taste

One 4- to 5-pound brisket

2 tablespoons peanut butter

2 cups water

3 tablespoons steak sauce

1½ cups dry white wine

1 tablespoon onion powder

1 teaspoon garlic powder

2 tablespoons olive oil

Salt and pepper the brisket real well and rub it in.

Put the peanut butter in a small pot with the water and cook over a low fire until the peanut butter melts. Add the steak sauce, then add the wine, onion powder, and garlic powder and stir well.

Preheat the oven to 325 degrees. Put the olive oil in a roaster pan and spread well over the bottom. Place the brisket in the roaster, then pour the peanut butter mixture around it, not on it. Cook for 1½ to 2 hours.

Mushroom Beef Brisket

MAKES 10 SERVINGS

One 6-pound brisket

Smoked salt to taste

Cayenne pepper to taste

3 to 4 garlic cloves, peeled

1 large onion, chopped

1 pound mushrooms, chopped

2 cups dry white wine

1½ cups water

2 tablespoons Worcestershire sauce

Rub the brisket all over with smoked salt and cayenne. Puncture the brisket with a small knife and stuff the holes with cloves of garlic. Place the brisket in an oiled roaster pan and toss the onion and mushrooms around it. Mix together the wine, water, and Worcestershire and pour around, not over, the brisket. Place in a preheated 350-degree oven and cook for 2 hours. Check with a kitchen fork to see if the brisket is cooked. If the liquid that comes out of the holes is bloody, cook for another 30 minutes.

Justin Wilson's Easy Cookin'

Boiled Brisket of Beef

MAKES 6 SERVINGS

One 3- to 5-pound beef brisket

Dried mint to taste

Louisiana hot sauce to taste

Soy sauce to taste

Garlic powder to taste

Onion powder to taste

I cup sliced mushrooms

Dried parsley to taste

Salt if needed

Put all the ingredients in a large pot and add enough water to cover the brisket. Bring to a boil, then reduce the fire to a simmer, and cook for 1½ hours.

Corned Beef and Cabbage

Dis is too good to talk about.

MAKES 8 SERVINGS, AT LEAST

One 5-pound corned beef

4 cups dry white wine

2 tablespoons soy sauce

**2 teaspoons Louisiana hot sauce or
    ¼ teaspoon cayenne pepper**

2 heads cabbage, cut into quarters

2 large onions, cut into quarters

Salt to taste

In a large pot, cover the corned beef with water. Stir in the wine, soy sauce, and hot sauce, bring to a boil, and boil until the brisket is tender, 2 to 3 hours, adding more water if you need to. Remove the corned beef to a plate.

Put the cabbage and onion quarters in the stock and boil until tender. Season with salt—but remember, the soy sauce has salt in it. Slice the corned beef and add to the cabbage and onions if you like, or serve separately.

Justin Wilson's Easy Cookin'

Cajun Boiled Dinner

There are all kinds of boiled dinners. There is something called New England boiled dinner, but dis certainly isn't dat. But I garontee everybody who cooks dis will enjoy it, I t'ink.

MAKES 8 SERVINGS

One 3-pound corned beef

½ cup chopped green onions

6 medium-size potatoes, peeled

2 bunches collard greens, washed real well, tough stems removed, and cut up

½ cup chopped bell peppers

½ cup chopped carrots

2 cups dry white wine

1 teaspoon chopped garlic

1 cup mushrooms with stems, chopped

Louisiana hot sauce to taste

Worcestershire sauce to taste

Salt to taste

Boil the corned beef according to the directions on the package. When cooked, remove from the pot and set aside. Add the remaining ingredients to the corned beef stock and cook until the carrots and potatoes are tender. Slice the beef and serve with the vegetables and broth.

Chili

1 cup corn flour

One 6-pack beer plus 1 extra can

Bacon drippings or olive oil

4 pounds chili meat, coarsely ground or cut
into small pieces

¼ cup chili powder

2 tablespoons unsweetened Hershey's cocoa
powder

3 cups chopped onions

1 cup chopped bell peppers

¼ cup chopped garlic

Salt to taste

1 cup chopped fresh parsley

In a medium-size mixing bowl, dissolve the corn flour as much as possible in 3 cans of the beer, stirring until smooth. Set aside.

Heat enough bacon drippings to coat the bottom of a large frying pan over a medium-high fire, then add the meat and brown it off. Add the remaining ingredients, including the dissolved corn flour, and let cook, covered, for at least an hour over a medium-low fire; it's best if you let it cook slowly for 3 hours.

Hominy and Chili Casserole

MAKES 8 SERVINGS

One 16-ounce can hominy, drained

1 cup chopped green onions

½ cup chopped bell peppers

½ cup dried parsley

1 tablespoon Worcestershire sauce

½ teaspoon dried mint

½ teaspoon garlic powder

1 cup dry white wine

Salt and cayenne pepper to taste

One 16-ounce can chili (no beans)

1 tablespoon olive oil

1 cup grated cheddar cheese

½ cup grated mozzarella cheese

¼ cup grated Parmesan or Romano cheese

Seasoned bread crumbs

Place the hominy, green onions, bell peppers, parsley, Worcestershire, mint, garlic powder, and wine in a medium-size pot and cook over a medium fire, stirring, until the onions and peppers are tender. Season with salt and cayenne and cook until most of the juice is gone.

Stir in the chili and pour into a casserole dish greased with the olive oil. Stir in the cheeses and top with the bread crumbs. Cook in a preheated 350-degree oven until the liquid is absorbed, about 1 hour.

Chili Jambalaya

MAKES 6 TO 8 SERVINGS

2 cups canned cooked chili

3 cups uncooked long-grain rice

1 cup mild picante sauce

One 12-ounce bottle nonalcoholic beer

2 teaspoons salt

1 cup water

Mix all the ingredients together in a 3-quart pot. Cook over a medium fire until most of the liquid is gone. Place the lid on the pot and reduce the fire to a simmer. Stir frequently and cook until the rice is done. Then reduce the fire to its lowest setting and let cook for 30 to 45 minutes without lifting the lid.

Cheese Hamburger Grits

MAKES 8 TO 10 SERVINGS

1 pound ground beef chuck

1 cup regular grits

5 cups water

2½ teaspoons salt

Louisiana hot sauce to taste

Worcestershire sauce to taste

1½ cups grated cheddar cheese

Garlic powder to taste

Mix all the ingredients together in a large saucepan and cook until the grits are firm, or the way you like them. Then put the mixture in the top of a double boiler, cover, and cook for about 1 hour over low heat.

Baked Pork Tenderloin

MAKES 10 SERVINGS

One 5½-pound pork tenderloin

1 cup fresh blueberries, picked over for
 stems

6 tablespoons pecan meal

Salt and cayenne pepper to taste

2 tablespoons olive oil

5 large Irish potatoes, peeled

2 tablespoons steak sauce

1 cup dry white wine

1 tablespoon finely chopped garlic

½ cup water

Cut a large pocket in the tenderloin and stuff the blueberries and 4 tablespoons of the pecan meal into it. Salt and pepper the loin and place in a roaster greased with the olive oil. Place the potatoes around the loin to hold the pocket closed. Dissolve the steak sauce in the wine and pour it around (not on) the loin, along with the garlic and water. Place the covered roaster in a preheated 300-degree oven and cook for 2½ hours.

Creole Mustard Pork Fingers

MAKES 6 SERVINGS

2 tablespoons olive oil

6 thick-cut pork fingers (boneless rib meat)

1 cup chopped onions

½ cup chopped bell peppers

1 cup chopped mushrooms of your choice

1 cup dry red wine (I like Chianti for this)

2 tablespoons chopped garlic

3 cups water

Louisiana hot sauce to taste

2 tablespoons Worcestershire sauce

2 teaspoons peanut butter melted in 1 cup
   boiling water

2 tablespoons Creole mustard

Salt to taste

Heat the oil in a large frying pan over a medium-high fire, brown the pork on both sides, and remove to a plate. Add the onions and bell peppers to the pan and cook, stirring, until softened, then add the mushrooms and wine, and then the pork, garlic, water, hot sauce, Worcestershire, peanut butter, and mustard. Season with salt and cook over a medium fire until the pork is done, stirring from time to time.

Fresh Pork and Sausage Jambalaya à la Party

MAKES 12 TO 20 SERVINGS

3 tablespoons olive oil

4 pounds boneless pork, cut into stew
    meat-size chunks

4 pounds smoked sausage, sliced

6 cups chopped onions

2½ cups chopped bell peppers

2 cups chopped fresh parsley

2 tablespoons chopped garlic

2 cups dry white wine

2 teaspoons dried mint

Salt and cayenne pepper to taste

1 cup mild picante sauce

1 cup steak sauce

12 cups water

6 cups uncooked long-grain rice

Heat the olive oil in a large pot over a medium-high fire and brown the pork on all sides, then remove to a plate. In the same pot, brown the sausage, then remove from the pot. Add the onions, bell peppers, and parsley to the pot and cook, stirring, over a medium fire until the onions are clear. Add the remaining ingredients except the meat and rice, bring to a boil, and add the meat. Bring to a boil again and add the rice. Cook until most of the water is gone.

Cover, reduce the fire to low, and simmer for 1 hour.

Justin Wilson's Easy Cookin'

Sausage Jambalaya

MAKES 10 TO 12 SERVINGS

2 tablespoons olive oil

3 pounds smoked sausage

2 cups chopped onions

1 cup chopped bell peppers

1½ cups chopped fresh parsley

4 cups uncooked long-grain rice

1½ to 2 cups dry white wine

1½ teaspoons chopped garlic

2 tablespoons Creole mustard

2 tablespoons Louisiana hot sauce

2 tablespoons Worcestershire sauce

Salt to taste

Heat the olive oil in a large pot, then brown off the sausage and remove to a plate. Add the onions, bell peppers, and parsley and cook, stirring, over a medium fire until the onions are clear. Add the rice, sausage, wine, and enough water to cover everything by ¾ inch. Stir in the garlic, mustard, hot sauce, and Worcestershire and season with salt. Cover the pot, reduce the fire to low, and cook until the rice is done, about 45 minutes.

Sausage Succotash

MAKES 8 TO 10 SERVINGS

½ cup olive oil

1 cup chopped onions

½ cup chopped bell peppers

1 cup chopped green onions

One 16-ounce can whole-kernel corn,
 drained

One 10-ounce can Rotel spiced tomatoes

One 16-ounce can whole or 1 pound fresh
 tomatoes, cut up

One 16-ounce can baby limas or butter
 beans, drained

1 cup water

2 teaspoons chopped garlic

1½ pounds smoked sausage, sliced

Heat the olive oil in a medium-size pot over a medium fire. Add the onions and bell peppers and cook, stirring, until the onions are clear, then add the rest of the ingredients and cook, covered, until everything is done, about 45 minutes.

Justin Wilson's Easy Cookin'

Macaroni, Sausage, and Pecan Casserole

Dis is great for a picnic.

MAKES 12 SERVINGS

1 pound small elbow macaroni

1½ cups shelled pecans

Salt to taste

½ teaspoon cayenne pepper

½ cup olive oil

½ cup dried parsley

1 teaspoon minced garlic

¾ pound pork sausage, cooked and thinly sliced

4 cups grated cheddar cheese

4 extra-large eggs, beaten

1 cup dry white wine

Bring a large pot of water to a boil, then add the macaroni, pecans, salt, cayenne, olive oil, parsley, and garlic and cook until the macaroni is done. Drain, then mix the macaroni, pecans, sausage, and 2 cups of the grated cheese together in a large bowl. Stir in the eggs and wine (seasoned with some cayenne) and mix together well.

Pour the mixture into a greased casserole dish, sprinkle over the remaining 2 cups grated cheese, and bake in a preheated 325-degree oven for 45 minutes.

Broccoli and Ham Casserole

For the broccoli:

8 cups broccoli (florets and stems cut into bite-size pieces)

1 pound slab bacon, cut up

2 teaspoons garlic powder

1 tablespoon onion powder

1 cup dry white wine

Salt and cayenne pepper to taste

For the casserole:

Olive oil

1 pound cooked smoked ham

2 cups grated cheddar cheese

½ cup grated Parmesan cheese

Place all the broccoli ingredients in a large pot with enough water to cover and bring to a boil, then reduce the fire to medium and cook until the broccoli is tender. Drain well.

Grease a casserole dish with olive oil. Combine the broccoli mixture with the ham in the casserole. Top with the cheeses and bake in a preheated 350-degree oven for about 45 minutes.

Lamb Patties

MAKES 6 SERVINGS

2 pounds ground lamb

½ cup dried parsley

Salt to taste

1 tablespoon onion powder

1 tablespoon white crème de menthe

1 teaspoon garlic powder

1 tablespoon picante sauce

Cayenne pepper to taste

1 large egg, beaten

Olive oil

Mix the lamb and parsley together in a large bowl with your hands. In a small bowl, beat the salt, onion powder, crème de menthe, garlic powder, picante sauce, and cayenne together with the egg real well. Add to the lamb, mix thoroughly by hand, and form into six patties.

Heat a generous coating of olive oil in a large frying pan. Fry several patties at a time until cooked the way you like them. Drain on paper towels.

Lamb and Ham Meat Loaf

2 pounds ground lamb

2 pounds ground ham (your butcher can
grind it for you)

½ cup pecan meal

2 cups chopped onions

¾ cup chopped bell peppers

1 teaspoon dried mint

2 teaspoons chopped garlic

4 large eggs, beaten

2 teaspoons salt

2 tablespoons steak sauce diluted in 1 cup
water

1 tablespoon Louisiana hot sauce

½ cup catsup

2 cups seasoned bread crumbs

2 tablespoons olive oil

1 cup dry white wine mixed with 1 cup water

Combine the two ground meats and the pecan meal, onions, bell peppers, mint, garlic, and beaten eggs in a large bowl. Combine the salt, steak sauce, hot sauce, and catsup in a small bowl, add to the meat, and mix well. Add the bread crumbs and combine thoroughly.

Preheat the oven to 350 degrees. Grease a roaster pan with the olive oil. Shape the mixture into two loaves and place them in the pan. Place in the oven for 10 minutes to firm up the loaves. Pour the wine and water around the loaves and cook at 325 degrees for 1½ to 2 hours, basting every 30 minutes.

Lamb-Potato Casserole

Dis is so good, whoooeee!

MAKES 8 SERVINGS

3 cups ground lamb, cooked in seasoned water to cover for 10 minutes and drained

4 cups mashed potatoes that have been cooked until tender in water seasoned with minced garlic and salt

2 tablespoons grated Parmesan cheese

Sliced sharp cheddar cheese to cover casserole

Mix the lamb and potatoes together well and put into an oiled casserole dish. Sprinkle with the Parmesan cheese and place the sliced cheddar on top. Bake in a preheated 300-degree oven for 45 minutes.

Rabbit Gumbo

MAKES 10 SERVINGS

1½ cups olive oil

1½ cups sifted all-purpose flour

2 cups chopped onions

½ cup chopped celery

1 cup chopped bell peppers

½ cup chopped fresh parsley

1 tablespoon chopped garlic

4 cups water

2 tablespoons steak sauce

Louisiana hot sauce to taste or 1 teaspoon
    cayenne pepper

2 cups dry white wine

One 2-pound rabbit, cut into serving pieces

1 pound andouille or smoked sausage

In a large pot, heat the oil over a medium fire, then add the flour and make a very dark roux (see my directions on page 49). Add the onions, celery, and bell peppers and cook, stirring constantly, until the onions are clear. Add the parsley, garlic, water, steak sauce, hot sauce, and wine, then drop in the rabbit meat and sausage. Stir to combine, then let cook, covered, for 2 or more hours.

Venison Roast

One 3-pound venison shoulder or ham roast

4 to 6 garlic cloves, peeled

Salt and cayenne pepper to taste

I pound mushrooms, sliced

2 cups chopped green onions

I cup chopped bell peppers

I cup dry red wine

I ½ cups water

2 tablespoons Worcestershire sauce

Be sure to remove all the fat from the venison. Puncture the roast all over with a small knife and stuff the garlic cloves into the holes. Rub the roast with salt and cayenne. Place the venison in an oiled roaster pan with a lid. Place the remaining ingredients around, not on, the roast, cover, and cook in a preheated 350-degree oven for about 2 hours. Baste the roast one time after an hour of cooking.

Smoking and Smokers

There are about as many different kinds of smokers as there are people. Most dedicated barbecuers make their own out of everything from an old refrigerator to a piece of gas pipeline. They are all good if they perform the basic purpose—to cook the meat slow and tender with a good smoke taste. I have several different types of smokers, but the three I use most are a Cajun Smoker, Cajun Microwave, and the Justin Wilson Novel Cooking Device.

Cajun Smoker There are several variations of this smoker, but basically it consists of six parts: the bottom container, the charcoal pan, the cylinder body, the top, the water pan, and the grills. You build the fire in the charcoal pan in the bottom container; put the water pan in the cylinder body and fill with hot water; set the cylinder body with the filled water pan on the bottom container with the charcoal pan filled with glowing charcoal to which has been added a wet wood of your choice;

insert the grill; place on the grill the meat or vegetables you are cooking; cover; and forget. All good Cajun Smokers contain instructions on how to use them and the amount of charcoal to use and the time required to properly cook meat or vegetables. The type of wood used varies; hickory is probably most frequently used. I like pecan. Apple, maple, and mesquite woods are also good. I generally use the Cajun Smoker for cooking smaller portions such as a turkey, chickens, or ribs.

Cajun Microwave This really works. The Cajun microwave is illustrated on page 113. You put your meat inside, slide the steel cover plate on top, and put hot charcoal or a wood fire on top of the steel plate. It cooks stuff in a hurry. It is especially good for cooking a pig and having a good time with friends.

Justin Wilson Novel Cooking Device This cooker/smoker was devised with a couple of good friends. It

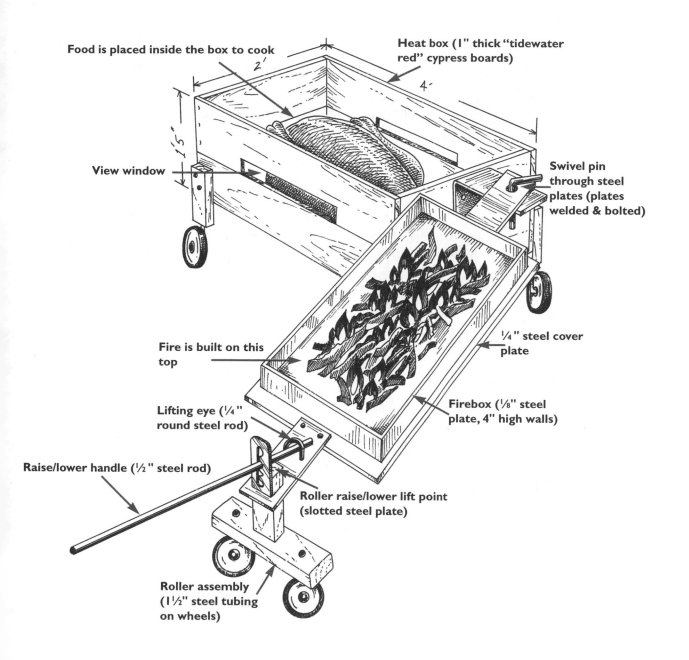

Food is placed inside the box to cook

Heat box (1" thick "tidewater red" cypress boards)

2'

4'

15"

View window

Swivel pin through steel plates (plates welded & bolted)

Fire is built on this top

¼" steel cover plate

Lifting eye (¼" round steel rod)

Firebox (⅛" steel plate, 4" high walls)

Raise/lower handle (½" steel rod)

Roller raise/lower lift point (slotted steel plate)

Roller assembly (1½" steel tubing on wheels)

Cajun Microwave

(not to scale)

is so unique and effective it has been patented. The basic features are that it can be used for smoking, roasting, baking, and can even be closed to obtain the same effect as a pressure cooker. The cooker is stainless steel and insulated with top vents that permit as much heat to escape or to be retained as desired. The most unique feature of the device is that it has two electrical cooking elements that are thermostat controlled in addition to a wood box at the lower right-hand side of the cooker. Thus, the ingredients in the cooking device can have the beneficial effect of the indirect smoke with a steady temperature provided by the thermostats on the electrical elements. Water pans are placed in the bottom to ensure sufficient moisture. The cooking device is excellent for preparing large quantities of food such as briskets, pigs, lamb, ribs, and chickens for a large crowd. One thing you have to be careful of is that if you do not provide enough vent for the cooker, it will cause the meat literally to fall from the bones.

Pork Loin

MAKES 6 TO 8 SERVINGS

Garlic powder to taste

Salt to taste

Cayenne pepper to taste

One 5½-pound bone-in pork loin roast

Build a fire on top of the Cajun microwave. Place a pan of water under the grill.

Pat the garlic powder, salt, and cayenne into the pork loin, place on the grill, and put the lid down. After about 2 hours, you can pull up the lid and stick a sharp fork in the meat to see how tender it is. Cook until the fork slides easily in and out.

Boston Butt

MAKES 10 TO 12 SERVINGS

One 9½-pound boneless Boston butt

Garlic powder to taste

Salt to taste

Cayenne pepper to taste

Build a fire on top of the Cajun microwave and place a pan of water under the grill.

Pat the meat with the garlic powder, salt, and cayenne, place on the grill, and put down the lid. Cook until fork-tender, 4 to 5 hours.

Leg of Lamb

MAKES 9 TO 11 SERVINGS

One 12½-pound leg of lamb

Garlic cloves, peeled

Garlic powder to taste

Salt to taste

Cayenne pepper to taste

Crème de menthe as needed

Build a fire on top of the Cajun microwave and place a pan of water under the grill.

Poke holes in the leg of lamb with a small sharp knife and stuff them with the garlic cloves. Pat the leg with the garlic powder, salt, and cayenne, then pour the crème de menthe over it and rub it into the lamb. Place the leg of lamb on the grill, pull down the lid, and cook until fork-tender, 5 to 8 hours.

Beef Brisket

MAKES 8 TO 12 SERVINGS

One 9½-pound beef brisket

Garlic powder to taste

Salt to taste

Cayenne pepper to taste

Build a fire in the Cajun microwave and place a pan of water under the grill.

Pat the brisket with the garlic powder, salt, and cayenne pepper. Place the brisket on the grill, pull the lid down, and cook until fork-tender, 5 to 6 hours.

Justin Wilson's Easy Cookin'

Rice and Beans

I love both rice and beans very much. In New Orleans, red beans and rice is served every Monday. However, the Cajuns prefer white beans usually, more than the reds. And there are many other beans jus' as good as any of those I mentioned, I garontee! Huh!

Chili Rice

Dis is a delightful dish. You can serve it by itself or with a good gravy or gumbo. It is so easy to fix, I garontee!

MAKES 4 TO 6 SERVINGS

2 cups uncooked long-grain rice

I tablespoon onion powder

2 teaspoons garlic powder

2 teaspoons salt

I tablespoon chili powder

2 tablespoons olive oil

Place all the ingredients except the oil in a large pot and cover with water to come up to the first joint of your middle finger. Pour the oil over the top (this will keep the water from boiling over). Bring to a boil and boil until most of the water is gone. Put the lid on the pot and reduce the fire to the lowest heat. Cook until the rice is done, about 45 minutes.

Rice with Cheese

If anybody comes and tries to lift the lid on dis, don' break their arm, but make them sorry they ever tried to lift dat lid.

MAKES 4 TO 6 SERVINGS

2 tablespoons olive oil

½ cup finely chopped onions

2 cups water

1½ cups uncooked long-grain rice

1 cup grated cheddar cheese

Salt to taste (about 1½ teaspoons)

Heat the olive oil in a medium-size pot over a medium fire, then add the onions and cook, stirring, until they are clear; do not brown. Pour the water over the onions, then add the rice and enough additional water to cover the rice by about 1 inch. Add the cheese and salt and stir in real good. Bring to a boil, stirring a couple of times. Reduce the fire to low, place a tight lid on the pot, and simmer until you can't see any water—45 minutes to 1 hour. Don't lift the lid for at least 45 minutes.

Justin Wilson's Easy Cookin'

Dilly Cheese Rice

I love dis rice.

MAKES 4 TO 6 SERVINGS

2 cups uncooked long-grain rice

½ cup grated cheddar cheese

1 tablespoon onion powder

1 teaspoon garlic powder

½ teaspoon dillweed

¼ teaspoon celery seed

2 teaspoons salt

½ teaspoon cayenne pepper

3 tablespoons olive oil

In a medium-size pot, combine all the ingredients except the oil. Add enough water to cover the rice and come up to the first joint of your middle finger, then pour the oil over the surface of the water (this will keep it from boiling over). Bring the water to a boil and continue to boil until craters form in the rice. Reduce the fire to low and cook, covered, for 30 to 45 minutes, until the rice is done.

Cheese Rice with Mushrooms

MAKES 4 TO 6 SERVINGS

2 cups uncooked long-grain rice

2 teaspoons salt

½ cup chopped mushrooms

1 tablespoon onion powder

1 teaspoon garlic powder

1 cup grated cheddar cheese

1 teaspoon cayenne pepper

3 tablespoons olive oil

Combine all the ingredients except the oil in a medium-size pot. Add water to cover the rice and come up to the first joint of your middle finger, then pour the olive oil over the surface of the water (this will keep it from boiling over). Bring to a boil and continue to boil until craters form in the rice. Reduce the fire to low, cover, and cook until the rice is done, 35 to 45 minutes.

Justin Wilson's Easy Cookin'

Mushroom Rice

MAKES 4 TO 6 SERVINGS

2 cups uncooked long-grain rice

I cup chopped mushrooms

2 teaspoons salt

I tablespoons onion powder

I teaspoon garlic powder

3 tablespoons olive oil

Combine all the ingredients except the oil in a medium-size pot and cover with water to come up to the first joint of your middle finger. Pour the oil over the surface of the water (this will keep it from boiling over). Cook over a medium fire until the water is just bubbling in craters in the rice. Reduce the fire to low, cover, and cook until the rice is done, about 30 minutes.

Pepper-Mushroom Rice

MAKES 4 TO 6 SERVINGS

2 cups uncooked long-grain rice

1½ teaspoons salt

2 tablespoons finely chopped onion

2 tablespoons finely chopped bell pepper

1 cup semi–finely chopped mushrooms

1 teaspoon chopped garlic

½ teaspoon cayenne pepper

2 tablespoons olive oil

Combine all the ingredients except the oil in a medium-size pot and cover with enough water to reach the first knuckle of your middle finger. Pour the olive oil over the surface of the water (this will keep it from boiling over). Bring to a boil and let boil until you can see craters in the rice. Reduce the fire to low, cover, and cook until the rice is done, about 30 minutes.

Wild Rice

Dis is the way we tame wild rice.

MAKES 4 TO 6 SERVINGS

2 cups uncooked wild rice

2 teaspoons salt

¼ teaspoon cayenne pepper

½ teaspoon garlic powder

1½ teaspoons onion powder

1 teaspoon dried mint

2 tablespoons olive oil

Combine all the ingredients except the oil in a medium-size pot and cover with an inch of water. Pour the oil over the surface of the water (this will keep it from boiling over). Bring to a boil and cook until most of the water is gone and there are little craters in the rice. Put the lid on the pot, reduce the fire to low, and let simmer for 45 minutes, stirring the rice occasionally.

Rice Dressing

Dis is a wondermous dressing and can be stuffed in a turkey, a hen, or a goose. If you don't want to do dat, jus' eat it like it is.

MAKES 8 TO 12 SERVINGS

2 tablespoons olive oil

1½ cups chopped onions

½ cup chopped bell peppers

½ cup chopped celery

½ cup chopped fresh parsley

1 tablespoon chopped garlic

2 pounds ground beef

1 pound ground pork

2 cups chicken stock

1 tablespoon Worcestershire sauce

Salt and cayenne pepper to taste

6 cups cooked long-grain rice

Heat the olive oil in a large frying pan over a medium fire. Add the onions, peppers, celery, and parsley and cook, stirring, until tender. Add the garlic and mix well. Cook for a few minutes, then add the beef and pork, stirring to mix them with the veggies. Cook, stirring, until mixed real well and the meat looks grayish. Add the stock and seasonings. Add the rice and mix well.

Place in an oiled casserole dish, cover, and bake in a preheated 350-degree oven for 45 minutes.

Red Beans and Rice Casserole

3 cups cooked red beans

3 cups cooked long-grain rice, seasoned with
   salt, garlic powder, onion powder, and
   olive oil to taste

1 cup cubed lean smoked ham

2 large eggs

½ cup dry white wine

Mild picante sauce to taste

Salt to taste

Sliced cheddar cheese to cover casserole

Combine the beans, rice, and ham in a large mixing bowl. Beat the eggs together in a small bowl and beat in the wine, picante sauce, and salt. Stir this into the rice-and-bean mixture, then transfer to an oiled casserole dish. Top with sliced cheddar cheese and bake in a preheated 300-degree oven for about 30 minutes.

Red Beans

MAKES 8 TO 10 SERVINGS

2 cups dried red beans, washed real well

1½ cups chopped onions

1 heaping teaspoon chopped garlic

1 cup dry white wine

1 pound pickled pork shoulder, fat removed
and cut into small pieces

1 teaspoon Liquid Smoke

½ cup dried parsley

1 teaspoon dried mint

1 tablespoon Louisiana hot sauce

1 tablespoon soy sauce

Salt to taste

Soak the beans for a few hours in water to cover in a large pot, then add all the other ingredients except the salt and bring to a hard boil. Reduce the fire to medium-low, cover, and cook until the beans are tender. Add the soy sauce and salt if needed.

Smoked Red Beans

2 cups dried red beans, washed real well

1 cup chopped onions

1 cup chopped bell peppers

1 teaspoon chopped garlic

½ teaspoon dried mint

2 teaspoons Liquid Smoke

1 tablespoon steak sauce

1 cup dry red wine

1 cup mushrooms, chopped

½ cup dried parsley

2 teaspoons Louisiana hot sauce

Salt to taste

Combine the first eight ingredients in a medium-size mixing bowl with water to cover and let them soak overnight.

Transfer the beans and soaking liquid to a medium-size pot and bring to a hard boil, then add the mushrooms, parsley, and hot sauce. Lower the fire to where there is just a bubble and cook until the beans are tender, then season with salt.

White Beans

MAKES 8 TO 10 SERVINGS

4 cups dried white beans, washed real well

I cup chopped onions

I cup chopped bell peppers

I tablespoon chopped garlic

2 teaspoons Liquid Smoke

I cup dried parsley

2 cups dry white wine

Salt to taste

Put the beans and water to cover by 2 to 3 inches in a large bowl. Let them soak at least 8 hours or overnight if possible. Drain the beans.

Combine the beans, onions, peppers, garlic, Liquid Smoke, and parsley in a large pot, then add the wine and cold water to cover. Cover the pot and bring to a boil. Cook over a low fire until beans mashed against the side of the pot are done. You may need to add more hot water before the beans finish cooking. Do not add the salt until the beans are tender.

Justin Wilson's Easy Cookin'

White Navy Beans

MAKES 6 SERVINGS

1 pound small navy beans, washed real well

2 cups chopped green onions

1 tablespoon chopped garlic

½ cup chopped celery

1 tablespoon dried parsley

½ teaspoon dried mint

¾ cup chopped bell peppers

½ pound pickled pork shoulder, fat removed
   and cut into small pieces

½ pound ham hocks

1 tablespoon Liquid Smoke

1 cup dry white wine

Louisiana hot sauce or cayenne pepper to
   taste

½ cup steak sauce

Salt to taste

Soak the first seven ingredients together in a large bowl overnight in enough water to generously cover the beans.

Pat the pickled pork dry with paper towels and brown it slightly in a large pot over a medium-high fire. Pour the beans and their soaking water into the pot with the meat and add the remaining ingredients except the salt. Bring to a boil, then cut down the heat to a nice bubbly boil. You may need to add hot water if the liquid cooks down. When the beans are more or less tender, season with salt if needed.

Beans Cooked in Corned Beef Stock

MAKES 4 TO 6 SERVINGS

1 pound dried red, pinto, white, or lima beans, washed real well

Corned Beef Stock (see page 135)

Soak the beans in water to cover for several hours, then drain.

In a large pot, bring enough stock to cover the beans to a boil, add the beans, bring back to a boil, and cook, covered, over a low fire until tender.

Corned Beef Stock

One 4-pound corned beef

1 tablespoon onion powder

2 teaspoons garlic powder

2 tablespoons Worcestershire sauce

Cayenne pepper to taste

Place the corned beef in a large pot and cover with water. Stir in the seasonings, cover, bring to a boil, and continue to boil for 1½ hours. Remove the corned beef from the stock. Use the stock to cook beans in.

Vegetables

I was reared on vegetables. When I was coming up, all our vegetables were grown on a truck farm. You will notice dat I cook mos' all vegetables real well and don' serve them half raw.

Mashed Potato Casserole

Olive oil

2 cups sliced onions

4 to 5 cups mushrooms, cut into large pieces

2 tablespoons soy sauce

2 teaspoons Louisiana hot sauce

½ cup dry white wine

6 cups mashed boiled and peeled potatoes

3 cups grated cheddar cheese

Heat enough olive oil to cover the bottom in a large ovenproof pan over a medium fire. Add the onions, then add the mushrooms, soy sauce, hot sauce, and wine and cook, stirring, until the onions and mushrooms are tender. Stir the potatoes into the sautéed mushroom mixture and cover with the grated cheese. Place in a preheated 350-degree oven for 20 minutes.

Mashed Garlic–Irish Potatoes Casserole

MAKES 6 SERVINGS

5 cups peeled and cut-up Irish potatoes

Onion powder to taste

Garlic powder to taste

Cayenne pepper to taste

2 cups grated cheddar cheese

Preheat the oven to 350 degrees. Boil the potatoes in water to cover, seasoned with onion and garlic powders and cayenne pepper, in a medium-size pot until tender. Drain and mash the potatoes. Place the potatoes in an oiled casserole dish and cover with the cheese. Bake, uncovered, for 30 minutes.

Potato Pancakes

2 cups all-purpose flour

1 teaspoon salt

1 teaspoon baking powder

1 teaspoon baking soda

1½ cups peeled and grated raw potatoes
   (do this in the food processor)

2 large eggs, well beaten

2 cups buttermilk

Olive oil

Mix the flour, salt, and baking powder and soda together in a large mixing bowl. Add the potatoes and mix well. Add the eggs and mix well. Add the buttermilk and mix well.

Generously coat the bottom of a large frying pan with olive oil and heat over a medium fire. Fry 4- to 5-inch pancakes until golden brown on both sides.

Hint: Keep your raw peeled potatoes in cool water until you food-process them. Then mix them into the rest of the ingredients as quickly as possible to keep them from turning brown.

Potato Pound Cakes

MAKES 6 SERVINGS

1 pound potatoes, peeled and grated

½ cup grated onions

1 cup corn flour

1 teaspoon baking soda

1 tablespoon salt

1 teaspoon cayenne pepper

3 large eggs, well beaten

1 cup buttermilk

2 tablespoons olive oil, heated

Olive oil for frying

Mix the potatoes and onions together in a large bowl real well. Mix in the corn flour, baking soda, salt, and cayenne. Add the eggs and mix, then add the buttermilk and mix well again. Add the heated oil and mix well.

Generously coat the bottom of a large frying pan with oil and heat over a medium fire. Fry 4- to 5-inch potato cakes until golden brown on both sides.

Justin Wilson's Easy Cookin'

Boiled Sweet Potatoes

Dat's so good I wish I had some right now.

4 cups chunks peeled sweet potatoes

1 teaspoon ground cinnamon

4 cups water

Salt to taste

Put all the ingredients in a medium-size pot and cover with a lid. Bring to a boil, reduce the fire to medium-low, and simmer until the potatoes are tender, about 30 minutes. You can serve them as is or mash them.

Mushrooms Sautéed in Olive Oil

MAKES 6 SERVINGS

½ cup olive oil

2 pounds mushrooms, sliced

1 cup dry white wine

2 tablespoons soy sauce

¼ teaspoon cayenne pepper

1 tablespoon fresh lemon juice

½ teaspoon garlic powder

1 teaspoon onion powder

½ teaspoon salt, if needed

Heat the olive oil in a large frying pan over a medium fire. Cook all the ingredients together, stirring, until the mushrooms are tender.

Eggs and Mushrooms and Onions

2 tablespoons olive oil

I cup chopped onions

I cup sliced mushrooms

3 large eggs

½ teaspoon garlic powder

Salt to taste

Heat the olive oil in a medium-size frying pan and cook the onions and mushrooms, stirring, until the onions are clear and the mushrooms are cooked. Beat the eggs, garlic powder, and salt together real well in a small bowl, then pour over the onions and mushrooms and cook, stirring, until the eggs are done. Serve over toast.

Boiled Corn

MAKES 6 SERVINGS

2 pounds slab bacon, cut into thick pieces

1 cup dry white wine

1 teaspoon cayenne pepper

Salt to taste

2 cups (4 sticks) butter or margarine

1 dozen ears sweet corn, shucked

Place the bacon, wine, cayenne, and salt in a large pot and pour in enough water to cover the corn when it is added. Bring to a rolling boil. Add the butter and let this cook for about 10 minutes. Bring to a rolling boil again and add the corn. Bring to a full boil again and cook for 20 minutes. Drain and serve.

Chicken Maque Chou

MAKES 8 SERVINGS

1 tablespoon bacon drippings (olive oil if
    you're worried about cholesterol)

¼ cup finely chopped onions

1 tablespoon chopped pickled jalapeño
    peppers

1 teaspoon finely chopped garlic

2 cups sweet corn cut and scraped off the
    cob or canned whole-kernel corn, drained

½ cup dry white wine

2½ to 3 pounds cooked chicken, meat cut
    into 1½-inch pieces (5 to 6 cups)

Salt to taste

Heat the bacon drippings in a large frying pan over a medium fire. Add the onions and cook, stirring, until clear. Add the jalapeños and cook, stirring, for 2 to 3 minutes. Add the garlic, then add the corn and wine. Add the chicken and cook until most all of the wine is gone. Season with salt and serve.

Maque Chou with Mushrooms

MAKES 8 TO 10 SERVINGS

1 cup olive oil

1½ cups chopped onions

1 cup chopped green onions

1 cup chopped bell peppers

1½ cups chopped fresh parsley

6 to 8 cups sweet corn cut and scraped off
   the cob

1 tablespoon chopped garlic

1½ cups dry white wine

1½ cups water

2 tablespoons steak sauce

2 tablespoons picante sauce

2 to 3 cups chopped mushrooms

Salt to taste

In a large frying pan, heat the olive oil over a medium fire. Add the onions, green onions, bell peppers, and parsley and cook, stirring, until the onions and bell peppers are tender. Add the corn and stir, then add the garlic, wine, and water and stir. Add the steak sauce and stir. Add the picante sauce and stir. Add the mushrooms and stir. Reduce the fire to low, cover, and simmer for about 1 hour. Add salt to taste.

Stewed Corn and Green Onions

MAKES 8 SERVINGS

¼ cup olive oil

8 cups chopped green onions

4 cups chopped onions

8 cups sweet corn cut and scraped off

   the cob

1 cup dry white wine

1 cup Rotel spiced tomatoes

1 cup water

2 teaspoons chopped garlic

Salt to taste

Combine all the ingredients in a large pot and cook over a medium fire for about 45 minutes, stirring often.

Stewed Corn and Mushrooms

MAKES 6 SERVINGS

2 tablespoons olive oil

I cup chopped onions

I½ cups chopped bell peppers

I cup chopped green onions

I cup finely chopped fresh parsley

2 cups chopped mushrooms

I teaspoon chopped garlic

I tablespoon Louisiana hot sauce

2½ tablespoons soy sauce

Salt to taste

4 cups sweet corn cut and scraped off
    the cob

I cup dry white wine

Heat the olive oil in a large frying pan over a medium fire. Add the onions and bell peppers and cook, stirring, until the onions are clear and the peppers are tender. Add the green onions and stir. Add the parsley and stir. Add the mushrooms and stir. Add the hot sauce, soy sauce, and salt and stir. Add the corn and wine and stir well. Reduce the fire to low, cover, and let simmer for 1 hour.

Green Onion Grits

I would like for people who don' know it dat dis is not jus' one grit. Dis is a lot of grits.

MAKES 6 SERVINGS

1 tablespoon margarine or butter

1 cup chopped green onions

5 cups water

2 teaspoons salt

½ teaspoon cayenne pepper

1 cup regular grits

Heat the margarine in the top of a double boiler directly over a medium fire. Add the green onions and cook, stirring, until tender. Add 1 cup of the water, bring to a boil, and let cook for about 5 minutes. Add the salt and cayenne, then add the remaining 4 cups water and the grits. Bring to a boil, stirring frequently. When the grits begin to thicken, place over the bottom of the double boiler, filled with simmering water, and continue to cook, stirring occasionally, covered, for 30 minutes.

Shiitake Mushrooms

MAKES 4 SERVINGS

½ cup olive oil

1 cup sliced shiitake mushroom caps

1 cup chopped onions

½ cup chopped bell peppers

2 teaspoons chopped garlic

½ cup dry white wine

1 tablespoon soy sauce

Heat the olive oil in a large frying pan over a medium fire. Add the mushrooms, onions, bell peppers, and garlic and cook, stirring, until the onions are clear. Add the wine and soy sauce and cook for 10 to 15 minutes longer.

Sautéed Shiitake Mushrooms and Onions

You can also eat dis by itself.

MAKES 4 TO 6 SERVINGS

Olive oil

1 cup sliced onions

1 cup sliced shiitake mushrooms

Soy sauce to taste

Salt and cayenne pepper to taste

Heat a little olive oil in a medium-size frying pan and cook all the ingredients over a medium fire, stirring, until the onions and mushrooms are tender. Serve over mashed potatoes, steak, or chicken.

Hominy and Mushrooms

MAKES 4 TO 6 SERVINGS

½ cup olive oil

½ cup chopped mushrooms

½ cup chopped onions

½ cup chopped bell peppers

½ cup chopped fresh parsley

Chopped garlic to taste

One 16-ounce can hominy

Heat the olive oil in a large frying pan over a medium fire. Add the remaining ingredients except the hominy and cook, stirring, until the onions are clear. Meanwhile, in another pan over a medium fire, cook all the water out of the hominy, then combine with the veggies. Cook, covered, for about 1 hour over a low fire.

Chinese Cabbage

Dis is good stuff.

2 cups dry white wine

2 teaspoons Liquid Smoke

2 tablespoons soy sauce

1 big head Chinese cabbage, coarsely cut up

½ teaspoon cayenne pepper

2 teaspoons salt

6 medium-size onions, chopped

2 teaspoons chopped garlic

6 cups water

Mix together the wine, Liquid Smoke, and soy sauce. Place the remaining ingredients in a large pot and stir the wine mixture into it. Cover and bring to a boil, then simmer over a low fire until the cabbage and onions are tender.

Boiled Cabbage
with Sweet Potatoes

MAKES 8 TO 10 SERVINGS

2 cups Brussels sprouts

4 cups 1-inch pieces peeled sweet potatoes

12 cups 1-inch cabbage cubes

1½ cups dry white wine

4 quarts water

Salt and cayenne pepper to taste

Place all the ingredients in a large pot. Bring to a boil and cook until the potatoes are tender.

Cabbage with Liquid Smoke

MAKES 6 SERVINGS

6 large mushrooms, sliced

2 large onions, roughly chopped

1 teaspoon Liquid Smoke

Salt to taste (about 2 teaspoons)

1 tablespoon Worcestershire sauce

½ teaspoon cayenne pepper

1 teaspoon chopped garlic

1 cup chopped bell peppers

1 cup dry white wine

1 medium-size head cabbage, cubed or
  shredded

Place all the ingredients except the cabbage in a large pot and cover well with water. Bring to a rolling boil, add the cabbage, and bring back to a boil. Lower the heat to a bubbly boil and cook until the cabbage, onions, and mushrooms are very tender, about 1 hour.

Okra and Crawfish and Mushrooms

Let's eat right now.

8 cups cut-up okra

2 cups canned chopped tomatoes

2 cups chopped mushrooms

2 cups chopped onions

1 cup dry white wine

2 cups mushroom stock (see Note)

2 teaspoons chopped garlic

1 pound crawfish tails, peeled

Combine all the ingredients except the crawfish in a medium-size pot over a medium fire and cook until the okra is tender. Stir in the crawfish tails and let cook for an additional 20 minutes.

Note: To make mushroom stock, take 1 pound cleaned whole mushrooms and boil them with 6 cups water until you have 2 cups stock left.

Stewed Okra and Eggplant

MAKES 6 TO 8 SERVINGS

3 tablespoons olive oil

1 cup chopped green onions

1 cup chopped onions

½ cup chopped bell peppers

4 cups ¼-inch-thick baby eggplant slices

2 pounds okra, chopped

2 teaspoons chopped garlic

2 tablespoons soy sauce

2 teaspoons Louisiana hot sauce or

   ¼ teaspoon cayenne pepper

Salt to taste (but remember, soy sauce is

   salty)

Heat the olive oil in a large frying pan over a medium fire. Add both kinds of onions and the bell peppers and cook, stirring, until the onions are clear. Add the eggplant, then add the remaining ingredients. Bring to a boil, then reduce to a low fire and cook until the eggplant is tender.

Eggplant Jambalaya

MAKES 12 SERVINGS

½ cup chopped celery

2 cups chopped onions

1 cup chopped fresh parsley

1 cup chopped bell peppers

1 cup chopped green onions

2 tablespoons chopped garlic

1 teaspoon cayenne pepper

2 tablespoons Worcestershire sauce

2 cups tomato sauce

1 cup dry white wine

Salt to taste

10 cups 1-inch cubes peeled eggplant

3 cups uncooked long-grain rice

Put all the ingredients except the eggplant and rice in a large pot and cover with water. Cook until the onions and bell peppers are tender.

Add the eggplant and enough water to cover the eggplant by ½ inch. Bring to a bubbly boil, then reduce the fire to medium-low and cook until the eggplant is tender. Add the rice, and be sure there is still ½ inch of water covering everything. Cook, uncovered, until most of the water is cooked out. Put the lid on the pot and simmer for 30 minutes.

Justin Wilson's Easy Cookin'

Eggplant and Tomatoes

MAKES 6 TO 8 SERVINGS

4 to 6 cups 1-inch cubes peeled eggplant

½ pound slab bacon, cut into 1-inch cubes

1 cup chopped onions

½ cup chopped bell peppers

½ teaspoon dried mint

½ cup dried parsley

1 cup dry white wine

1 tablespoon minced garlic

2 tablespoons soy sauce

1 tablespoon Louisiana hot sauce or
    ½ teaspoon cayenne pepper

4 to 6 cups cubes peeled fresh tomatoes

Cook the eggplant in salted water to cover until tender; drain.

In a large frying pan, fry the bacon cubes until crisp. Add the onions and bell peppers and cook over a medium fire, stirring, until the onions are clear. Add the mint, parsley, and wine, then add the rest of the ingredients, including the drained eggplant. Bring to a boil, reduce to a low fire, cover, and cook for 1½ hours. Serve over toast.

Eggplant Justin

Dese is so good it ought to be a law to cook dem.

For the eggplant:

6 to 8 medium-size eggplant, unpeeled, sliced lengthwise in half

2 cups dry white wine

Salt to taste (about 1 tablespoon)

3 cups chopped bell peppers

For the crawfish:

2 pounds crawfish tails, peeled

½ cup (1 stick) margarine or butter

4 cups chopped onions

2 cups chopped green onions

1½ cups chopped fresh parsley or ¾ cup dried parsley

1 tablespoon fresh lemon juice

1 tablespoon steak sauce

1 tablespoon minced garlic

1 teaspoon dried mint

Salt to taste

Louisiana hot sauce or cayenne pepper to taste

1 to 2 cups seasoned bread crumbs

Combine the eggplant ingredients and water to cover in a large pot and bring to a boil, then simmer until the eggplant is tender. Let cool, then very carefully remove the eggplant meat from the shells. There should be 4 cups of eggplant meat. In a large bowl, mash the eggplant to get most of the lumps out.

Bring the crawfish ingredients, except the bread crumbs, and water to cover to a boil in another large pot and let boil for 30 minutes. Add the mashed eggplant to the crawfish mixture and cook, covered, over a low fire for 15 minutes. Add some bread crumbs (how much depends on how juicy you want this mixture to be). Place the mixture in an oiled casserole dish and sprinkle more bread crumbs on top. Place in a preheated 350-degree oven for 10 to 15 minutes.

Pork Backbone and Turnips

Dis dish is unbelievably tasty. In fact, I knew a man once and I could tell him I was cooking dis dish and he would quit his job to come eat it.

MAKES 8 TO 12 SERVINGS

2 tablespoons olive oil

3 cups chopped onions

2 cups chopped green onions

1½ cups chopped bell peppers

1 cup chopped celery

1 cup chopped fresh parsley

2 teaspoons garlic powder

2 tablespoons peanut butter melted in
  2 cups boiling water

1½ cups Sunsweet Lighter Bake

1 cup dry white wine

2 cups chopped mushrooms

2 tablespoons Louisiana hot sauce

1 tablespoon salt, or as much as you like

6 cups peeled and chopped turnips

One 2¼-pound pork backbone, bones
  separated

Heat the olive oil in a large pot over a medium fire. Add the onions, green onions, bell peppers, celery, and parsley and cook, stirring, until the vegetables are tender. Add the garlic powder, melted peanut butter, and Sunsweet Lighter Bake. Stir in the wine and mushrooms and cook for about 15 minutes.

Add the hot sauce and salt. Bring to a boil, then add the turnips and bring back to a boil. Let cook, covered, for about 15 minutes, then add the pork and bring back to a boil. Lower the fire to a simmer and cook, covered, for 2 hours, stirring every 10 or 15 minutes.

No-Fat Kale

MAKES 6 SERVINGS

1 cup chopped onions

1½ teaspoons chopped garlic

1 teaspoon dried mint

1 tablespoon smoked salt, or as much as
   you like

1 tablespoon Liquid Smoke

1 cup dry white wine

1 tablespoon Worcestershire sauce

2 teaspoons Louisiana hot sauce

3 bunches kale, washed real well and tough
   stems removed

Half-fill a pot that is large enough to hold the kale with water and add all the ingredients except the kale. Bring to a rolling boil, then add the kale a little at a time, stirring it into the water. Cook until the kale is tender and tasty. Taste for salt.

Mustard Greens

I love dis. And it's good for me too.

¾ pound salt pork, cut into pieces

1½ cups chopped onions

6 cups water

1 heaping teaspoon minced garlic

1 cup dry white wine

4 big bunches mustard greens, washed real
   well and tough stems removed

1 tablespoon Louisiana hot sauce

2 tablespoons soy sauce

Salt to taste

In a large pot, cook the salt pork, stirring, over a medium fire until it renders up its fat. Add the onions, water, garlic, and wine. Bring to a boil, then add the mustard greens a little at a time, stirring them into the liquid. Stir in the hot sauce and soy sauce. Cook until tender, then season with salt if needed.

Smoked Mustard Greens

MAKES 6 SERVINGS

1 cup chopped onions

2 teaspoons finely chopped garlic

1 teaspoon dried mint

1 cup dry white wine

3 or 4 smoked pork neck bones

1 tablespoon Worcestershire sauce

1 tablespoon Louisiana hot sauce or

   1 teaspoon cayenne pepper

3 to 4 bunches mustard greens, washed real

   well, tough stems removed, and chopped

Salt to taste

Place the onions, garlic, and mint in a large pot of water with the wine mixed in. Add the neck bones, Worcestershire, and hot sauce. Bring to a boil and cook for about 10 minutes. Add the chopped greens, season with salt, and cook until tender.

Stewed Kumquats

Dis is so good you can overeat it.

MAKES 6 CUPS

4 cups kumquats, mashed real good with a
　　heavy dinner fork

½ cup honey

½ cup brandy

I teaspoon vanilla extract

I cup Chablis wine

I cup water

I teaspoon ground cinnamon

Combine all the ingredients in a medium-size pot. Bring to a boil, cover, and let cook over a low fire until thickened, like a jam.

Sauces

Sauces are good to help the flavor of any fish or meat you may be cookin'. The basting and barbecue sauces are necessary if you're going to be a success at the grill or smoker.

Tartar Sauce I

MAKES ABOUT 7¾ CUPS

4 cups mayonnaise

½ cup horseradish sauce

3 tablespoons olive oil

1 cup dill relish, drained

1 cup sweet relish, drained

1 cup finely chopped onions

½ teaspoon cayenne pepper

1 tablespoon Worcestershire sauce or

  ½ teaspoon Worcestershire powder

1 teaspoon garlic powder

Place the mayonnaise and horseradish in a large mixing bowl and beat with a whisk until fully mixed. Add the olive oil, slowly beating with a whisk until the original mayonnaise consistency returns. Add the rest of the ingredients one at a time, beating or stirring after each addition. Will keep covered in the refrigerator for several weeks.

Tartar Sauce II

MAKES ABOUT 1¾ CUPS

1½ cups mayonnaise

2 teaspoons sweet onion relish, well drained

2 teaspoons sweet relish, well drained

2 teaspoons dill relish, well drained

2 teaspoons creamy-style horseradish sauce

1 teaspoon dillweed

¼ teaspoon garlic powder

¼ teaspoon cayenne pepper

Mix all the ingredients together real well. Will keep covered in the refrigerator for several weeks.

Rémoulade Sauce

2 cups mayonnaise

One 10-ounce bottle Durkee's Famous Sauce

½ cup olive oil

1 cup Creole or Grey Poupon mustard

½ cup horseradish sauce

1 cup catsup

1 tablespoon red wine vinegar

2 tablespoons steak sauce

2 tablespoons mild picante sauce

Salt if needed

Mix together the mayonnaise and Durkee's, then pour in the olive oil and beat until it returns to the consistency of the mayonnaise. Add the mustard and beat some more. Add the horseradish and beat some more. Add the catsup and beat some more. Beat in the vinegar. Then add the steak sauce, beating all the time. Add the picante sauce, and beat some more. Season with salt if needed. Will keep covered in the refrigerator for several weeks.

Barbecue Sauce I

MAKES 1 GALLON

1 cup peanut oil

4 to 5 cups chopped onions, processed to a
    liquid in a food processor

1 cup chopped celery

1½ cups chopped fresh parsley

2 cups chopped bell peppers

1 cup peanut butter melted in 1 cup boiling
    water

3 tablespoons chopped garlic

3 cups steak sauce

3 cups catsup

2 teaspoons cayenne pepper

1 tablespoon salt, or as much as you like

1½ cups tequila

Heat the peanut oil in a 6- to 8-quart pot. Add the onions, celery, parsley, and bell peppers and cook over a medium fire, stirring, until the onions are clear. Add the melted peanut butter and stir. Add the garlic, steak sauce, and catsup, stirring after each addition. Add the cayenne and salt, then add the tequila. Bring to a boil, then cook, covered, over a low fire for several hours, stirring frequently. Will keep covered in the refrigerator for several weeks.

Justin Wilson's Easy Cookin'

Barbecue Sauce II

1 cup olive oil

4 to 5 cups chopped onions, processed to a
liquid in a food processor

1 cup chopped celery

1½ cups chopped fresh parsley

2 cups chopped bell peppers

2 tablespoons peanut butter melted in
1½ cups boiling water

3 cups steak sauce

3 cups catsup

2 teaspoons cayenne pepper

Salt to taste

1 cup amaretto

Heat the olive oil in a 6- to 8-quart pot. Add the onions, celery, parsley, and bell peppers and cook over a medium fire, stirring, until the onions are clear. Add the melted peanut butter and stir, then add the steak sauce and catsup, stirring after each addition. Add the cayenne and salt, then add the amaretto. Bring to a boil, then cook, covered, over a low fire for several hours, stirring frequently. Will keep covered in the refrigerator for several weeks.

Diabetic Barbecue Sauce

MAKES 1 GALLON

2 tablespoons olive oil

1 cup liquefied (in a food processor) onions
  (1½ cups chopped)

1 cup liquefied fresh parsley (1½ cups
  chopped)

1 cup liquefied bell peppers (1½ cups
  chopped)

1 tablespoon chopped garlic, liquefied in a
  food processor

1 cup liquefied fresh tomatoes

2 teaspoons Equal dissolved in 1 cup water

2 teaspoons dry mustard dissolved in 1 cup
  water

1 cup fresh lemon juice

1 teaspoon dried mint

1 cup pitted black olives, drained and
  liquefied in a food processor

2 tablespoons sugar-free soy sauce

¼ to ½ teaspoon cayenne pepper, as you
  like it

2 teaspoons salt

Heat the olive oil in a large saucepan, then add the pureed onions, parsley, bell peppers, and garlic and cook, uncovered, over a medium fire, stirring occasionally, for about 30 minutes.

Add the rest of the ingredients and cook, covered, for at least 2 hours over a low fire, stirring every now and then. Will keep covered in the refrigerator for several weeks.

Basting Sauce

This works with just about anything.

MAKES ABOUT 1 QUART

2 cups dry white wine or 1 cup crème de
    menthe

2 cups water

2 tablespoons fresh lemon juice

Dried mint to taste

Salt to taste

Garlic powder to taste

Mix everything together and use or you can keep covered in the refrigerator for up to one month.

Basting Sauce for Beef and Pork

MAKES ABOUT 3 CUPS

1 cup dry light red wine (I like to use
   Chianti)

2 cups water

1 tablespoon fresh lemon juice

1 tablespoon onion powder

½ teaspoon cayenne pepper or 1 tablespoon
   picante sauce

1 teaspoon garlic powder

Mix all the ingredients together and baste the cooking meat as needed. Will keep in the refrigerator covered for several weeks.

Basting Sauce for Lamb and Venison

1 cup crème de menthe

1 cup dry light red wine (I like to use
   Chianti)

½ teaspoon garlic powder

1 cup water

1 teaspoon onion powder

½ teaspoon dried mint

1 tablespoon fresh lemon juice

Mix all the ingredients together and baste the cooking meat as needed. Will keep in the refrigerator covered for up to one month.

Desserts

You will notice dat dere are a lot of cobblers and dat dey are put together in a very easy way. I've also included a nice rice pudding dat I like very much, and a bread pudding too. Dat's enough pudding desserts—I don' care what anybody says.

Blackberry Cobbler

MAKES 8 TO 10 SERVINGS

For the filling:

2 cups dry white wine

1 teaspoon ground cinnamon

1 teaspoon vanilla extract

1 cup honey

½ cup brandy

8 cups fresh blackberries, picked over

For the crust:

½ cup (1 stick) margarine or butter, softened

¾ cup sugar

1½ cups all-purpose flour

1 teaspoon baking powder

¾ teaspoon salt

1½ cups apple and pineapple juices
   combined

Preheat the oven to 350 degrees. To prepare the filling mix together all the ingredients except the berries and pour over the berries in a medium-size saucepan. Bring to a boil, then simmer over a low fire until the berries are soft, about 5 minutes. Pour the mixture into a buttered deep 9 × 12-inch casserole dish and set aside.

To prepare the crust, in a medium-size mixing bowl, cream the margarine with the sugar, then add the flour, baking powder, salt, and fruit juices and mix well. Pour the batter over the blackberry mixture and bake until golden brown, about 1 hour.

Strawberry Cobbler

MAKES 8 TO 10 SERVINGS

For the filling:

½ cup (1 stick) margarine or butter

1 cup sugar

2 tablespoons all-purpose flour

¼ teaspoon salt

4 pints fresh strawberries, hulled and sliced

¾ cup brandy

For the crust:

½ cup (1 stick) margarine or butter, softened

½ cup sugar

1½ cups all-purpose flour

2 teaspoons baking powder

½ teaspoon salt

½ to 1 cup pineapple juice

Preheat the oven to 350 degrees. To prepare the filling, melt the margarine in a medium-size saucepan over a medium fire.

Stir in the sugar, flour, and salt and mix well. Add the strawberries and brandy, stir, and heat thoroughly, about 5 minutes. Pour the mixture into a buttered deep 9 × 12-inch casserole dish and set aside.

To prepare the crust, in a medium-size mixing bowl, cream the margarine with the sugar, then add the flour, baking powder, salt, and enough pineapple juice so the batter can pour; mix well. Pour the batter over the strawberries and bake until golden brown, about 1 hour.

Justin Wilson's Easy Cookin'

Blueberry Cobbler

For the filling:

½ cup (1 stick) margarine or butter

1½ cups sugar

2 tablespoons all-purpose flour

½ teaspoon salt

9 cups fresh blueberries, picked over for
   stems

¾ cup brandy or water

For the crust:

½ cup (1 stick) margarine or butter, softened

¾ cup sugar

1½ cups all-purpose flour

1 teaspoon baking powder

¾ teaspoon salt

1½ cups apple or pineapple juice or milk

Preheat the oven to 350 degrees. To prepare the filling, melt the margarine in a medium-size saucepan over a medium fire. Stir in the sugar, flour, and salt and mix well. Add the blueberries and water, stir, and heat thoroughly, about 5 minutes. Pour the mixture into a buttered deep 9 × 12-inch casserole dish and set aside.

To prepare the crust, in a medium-size mixing bowl, cream the margarine with the sugar, then add the flour, baking powder, salt, and fruit juice and mix well. Pour the batter over the blueberries and bake until golden brown, about 1 hour.

Peanut Butter–Blueberry Cobbler

MAKES 8 TO 10 SERVINGS

For the filling:

1 cup (2 sticks) margarine or butter

1 cup sugar

¼ cup all-purpose flour

½ teaspoon salt

6 cups fresh blueberries, picked over for
    stems

1 cup brandy

For the crust:

½ cup (1 stick) margarine or butter, softened

¾ cup sugar

3 cups all-purpose flour

1 tablespoon baking powder

½ teaspoon salt

1 cup pineapple juice

1 tablespoon peanut butter melted in 1 cup
    boiling water

Preheat the oven to 350 degrees. To make the filling, melt the margarine in a large saucepan over a medium fire. Stir in the sugar, flour, and salt and mix well. Add the blueberries and brandy, mix well, and heat thoroughly, about 5 minutes. Pour into a buttered deep 9 × 12-inch baking or casserole dish and set aside.

To prepare the crust, cream the margarine with the sugar in a medium-size mixing bowl. Add the flour, baking powder, and salt, then add the juice and melted peanut butter and mix well. Pour the batter over the blueberry mixture and bake until golden brown, about 1 hour.

Justin Wilson's Easy Cookin'

Peach Cobbler

MAKES 8 TO 10 SERVINGS

For the filling:

½ cup (1 stick) margarine or butter

1 cup sugar

3 tablespoons corn flour

¼ teaspoon salt

1 teaspoon ground cinnamon

10 ripe peaches, peeled, pitted, and thinly
   sliced

½ cup brandy or water

For the crust:

½ cup (1 stick) margarine or butter, softened

½ cup sugar

1½ cups corn flour, sifted

1 cup pecan meal, sifted

1½ teaspoons baking powder

½ teaspoon salt

1 cup milk or water

Preheat the oven to 350 degrees. To prepare the filling, melt the margarine in a large saucepan over a medium fire. Stir in the sugar, corn flour, salt, and cinnamon and mix well. Add the peaches and brandy, stir, and heat thoroughly, about 5 minutes. Pour into a buttered deep 9 × 12-inch casserole dish and set aside.

To prepare the crust, in a medium-size mixing bowl, cream the margarine with the sugar, then add the corn flour, pecan meal, baking powder, salt, and milk and mix well. Pour the batter over the peaches and bake until golden brown, about 1 hour.

Apricot Cobbler

For the filling:

½ cup (1 stick) margarine or butter

1½ cups sugar

3 tablespoons all-purpose flour

¼ teaspoon salt

15 to 20 ripe apricots, pitted and sliced

1 cup brandy

For the crust:

½ cup (1 stick) margarine or butter, softened

¾ cup sugar

1½ cups all-purpose flour

1 cup pecan meal

1 tablespoon baking powder

¾ teaspoon salt

1 large egg

⅔ cup pineapple juice

⅔ cup apple juice

Preheat the oven to 350 degrees. To prepare the filling, melt the margarine in a large saucepan over a medium fire. Stir in the sugar, flour, and salt and mix well. Add the apricots and brandy and stir until heated thoroughly, 5 to 8 minutes. Pour into a buttered deep 9 × 12-inch baking pan or casserole dish. Set aside.

To prepare the topping, in a medium-size mixing bowl, cream the margarine with the sugar, then add the flour, pecan meal, baking powder, and salt. Beat the egg with the fruit juices, then add it to the other ingredients and mix well. Pour the batter over the apricots and bake until golden brown, about 1 hour.

Apple Cobbler

For the filling:

½ cup (1 stick) margarine or butter

1 cup sugar

2½ tablespoons corn flour

¼ teaspoon salt

1½ teaspoons ground cinnamon

¾ cup brandy

6 large red Delicious apples, cored, peeled,
   and thinly sliced

For the crust:

½ cup (1 stick) margarine or butter, softened

½ cup sugar

½ cup corn flour, sifted

¾ cup pecan meal, sifted

1 teaspoon baking powder

½ teaspoon salt

1 cup pineapple juice or water

Preheat the oven to 350 degrees. To prepare the filling, melt the margarine in a large saucepan over a medium fire. Stir in the sugar, corn flour, and salt and mix well. Stir in the cinnamon, brandy, and apples, mix well, and heat thoroughly, about 5 minutes. Pour into a buttered deep 9 × 12-inch baking or casserole dish. Set aside.

To prepare the crust, in a medium-size mixing bowl, cream the margarine with the sugar, then add the corn flour, pecan meal, baking powder, salt, and fruit juice and mix well. Pour the batter over the apples and bake until golden brown, about 1 hour.

Strawberry Pie

MAKES TWO 9½-INCH PIES

1 pint fresh strawberries, hulled and sliced

¾ cup sugar mixed with 1 teaspoon ground
  cinnamon

2 cups chopped walnuts

Two 9½-inch unbaked pie shells

Toss the strawberries with the sugar-
and-cinnamon mixture in a medium-
size mixing bowl and let sit, covered, in
the refrigerator overnight.

Toast the walnuts in a skillet over a
medium fire until they begin to brown.

Preheat the oven to 400 degrees. Divide
the strawberries between the pie shells
and sprinkle the walnuts over the top of
each. Place the pies in the oven for
5 minutes, then lower the oven
temperature to 325 degrees and bake for
30 minutes. Let cool, then place in the
refrigerator overnight, or for at least
6 hours, before serving.

Walnut Pie

4 large eggs

1 cup sugar

2 tablespoons margarine or butter, melted

¼ cup all-purpose flour

1½ cups sugar cane molasses

1½ teaspoons vanilla extract

¾ teaspoon salt

3 cups walnuts, chopped

Two 9½-inch unbaked pie shells

Preheat the oven to 350 degrees. In a large mixing bowl, beat the eggs, then gradually beat in the sugar, margarine, and flour. Beat in the molasses, vanilla, and salt. Stir in the walnuts and mix well. Divide the filling between the unbaked pie shells and bake until firm in the middle, about 1 hour.

Bread Pudding

MAKES 12 SERVINGS

1 loaf stale white bread

4 large eggs

1½ cups sugar

1 cup brandy

3 cups milk

1 tablespoon vanilla extract

2 cups raisins

Peanut oil

Preheat the oven to 350 degrees. Break the bread into chunks into a large mixing bowl. In another bowl, beat the eggs. Add the sugar and brandy to the beaten eggs, then add the milk and beat well. Mix in the vanilla and raisins and pour the mixture over the bread. Mix all the ingredients together and let sit until the liquid has soaked into the bread, mixing two or three times.

Turn the bread mixture into a 9 × 12-inch casserole or baking dish oiled with peanut oil and bake until a toothpick inserted in the middle comes out dry, 30 to 45 minutes.

You do not need rum sauce for this pudding. Serve with vanilla ice cream on top.

Brown Rice Pudding

MAKES 12 SERVINGS

2 cups dry white wine

1 cup honey

1 teaspoon vanilla extract

1 teaspoon ground cinnamon

2 cups raisins

4 extra-large eggs

8 cups cooked brown rice

Combine the wine, honey, vanilla, and cinnamon in a medium-size saucepan. Heat slowly over a low fire until the honey melts, then add the raisins and bring to a boil. Remove from the heat and let cool for about 30 minutes.

Preheat the oven to 325 degrees. Beat the eggs real well and combine with the rice in a large mixing bowl. Pour the honey-and-wine mixture over the rice and combine well. Butter a 9 × 12-inch baking pan, then pour in the pudding mixture. Bake until browned, about 1 hour. Keep an eye on it, and don't let it burn.

Index